Mastering
Algorithms with C

Perfect Beginner's Guide 2014.

Harry H. Chaudhary.
(IT Manager @ Anonymous International)

Author Note:

Every possible effort has been made to ensure that the information contained in this book is accurate, and the publisher or the Author can't accept responsibility for any errors or omissions, however caused.

All liability for loss, disappointment, negligence or other damage caused by the reliance of the Technical Programming or other information contained in this book, of in the event of bankruptcy or liquidation or cessation of trade of any company, individual; or firm mentioned, is hereby excluded.

All other marks are property of their respective owners. The examples of companies, organizations, products, domain names, email addresses, logos, people, places, and events depicted herein are fictitious. No association with any real company, organization, product, domain name, email address, logo, person, place, or event is intended or should be inferred.

The author and publisher have taken care in the preparation of this book, but make no expressed or implied warranty of any kind and assume no responsibility for errors or omissions. No liability is assumed for incidental or consequential damages in connection with or arising out of the use of the information or programs contained herein.

This book expresses the author views and opinions. The information contained in this book is provided without any express, statutory, or implied warranties. Neither the authors, and Publisher, nor its resellers, or distributors will be held liable for any damages caused or alleged to be caused either directly or indirectly by this book.

ISBN 13: **978-1500137137.**
ISBN-10: **1500137138.**

Printed & Published By Createspace O-D Publishing LLC- USA.
Marketing & Distribution By Amazon Inc. & Other 1500 worldwide Bookstores.

Dedication

"This book is dedicated to all those who make the daily sacrifices,

Especially those who've made sacrifice, to ensure our freedom & security."

Thanks to Lord Shiva a lot for giving me the technical and all abilities in my life to write.

Dear Dad, Thank you baauji for teaching me by example what it means to live a life based on principles.

Dear Mom, Thank you for showing me in a real way how to live according to the most imp. principle, and unconditional love.

Dear Sisters & Brother (Mohit Para Military Commando), Thank you, your smile brightens my every day. Your zest makes my heart sing. I love You more than I can say .

I would especially like to mention the name of beautiful faces inside my life who helped me in coping with my sorrows:

Thank you Priyanka, you are the meaning of my life and apple of my eyes, I Love You more than I can say.

Thank you Navneet, Mary Lou and Eminem - you are the inspiration you made me like "Sing for the movement" again,

Thanks to all Hackers And Communities including my Enemies.

In Loving Memories of My Loved One –My Uncle Lt. G.C

In Loving Memories of My Loved One –My Lt. Grand Mom.

You told me that everything will be okay in the end,
You also told me that, if it's not okay, it's not the end.
"I'll search for you through 1000 worlds & 10000 lifetimes until I find you"

About Author:

Harry, H. Chaudhary is an Indian computer Programming and Bestselling Java Author and **scientifically Hacking professional** has a unique experience in the field of computers Programming, **Hacking and Cyber Security.**

He has helped many Countries Governments and many multinational Software companies of around the globe to secure their networks and securities. He has authored several books on Various Computers Programming Languages and computer security & Hacking. He is basically known for his international bestselling Programming book "Core Java Professional."

He is technically graduate software engineer and Master. He is the leading authority on C Programming and C++ Programming as well as on Core Java and Data Structure and Algorithms. His acclaimed C and C++ & Java books. He has over 5 years of experience as a software methodologist. His teaching and research interests are in the areas of artificial intelligence, programming languages.

He is living two lives. One life, He is a Computer program writer for a respectable software company. The other life is lived in computers, where he go by the hacker alias 'Harry" and are guilty of virtually every computer crime. Currently he is working as offline IT manager @ world famous community **Anonymous international Community.**

Author side :

You may have noticed something missing here: no impressive of credentials. I haven't been a professor at a Prestigious University for a quarter-century; neither am I a top executive at a Silicon Valley giant. In some ways, I'm a student of Technology, just like you are.

And my experience over the years has shown me that many of the people who know the most about how technology works also have rather limited success in explaining what they know in a way that will allow me to understand it. My interests, and I believe my skills, lie not in being an expert, but an educator, in presenting complex information in a form that is sensible, digestible and fun to read my books.

"What is real? How do you define *real*? If you're talking about what you can feel, what you can smell, what you can taste and see, then real is simply, electrical signals interpreted by your brain."

"... I am just now beginning to discover the difficulty of expressing one's ideas on paper. As long as it consists solely of description it is pretty easy; but where reasoning comes into play, to make a proper connection, a clearness & a moderate fluency, is to me, as I have said, a difficulty of which I had no idea ..."

– Harry

Contents

Preface

∞ **Essential DSA Skills--Made Easy!** ∞

This book gives a good start and Complete introduction for data structures and algorithms for Beginner's. While reading this book it is fun and easy to read it. This book is best suitable for first time DSA readers, Covers all fast track topics of DSA for all Computer Science students and Professionals.

Data Structures and Other Objects Using C or C++ takes a gentle approach to the data structures course in C Providing an early, text gives students a firm grasp of key concepts and allows those experienced in another language to adjust easily. Flexible by design,. Finally, a solid foundation in building and using abstract data types is also provided.

Using C, this book develops the concepts and theory of data structures and algorithm analysis in a gradual, step-by-step manner, proceeding from concrete examples to abstract principles. Standish covers a wide range of Both traditional and contemporary software engineering topics.

This is a handy guide of sorts for any computer science engineering Students, *Data Structures And Algorithms* is a solution bank for various complex problems related to data structures and algorithms. **It can be used as a reference manual by Computer Science Engineering students. this Book also covers all aspects of B.TECH CS, IT, and BCA and MCA, BSC IT.**

CHAPTER

∞ 1 ∞

(Introduction of DSA)

Introduction-

A data structure is a collection of data items stored in memory; in addition a number of operations are provided by the software to manipulate that data structure.

A data structure means there is a relationship of some kind between data items, exactly what the relationship are determine what type of data structure is being used.

Data:

The term data simply refers to a value or a set of values. These values may represent some observation from an experiment, some figures collected during some survey (such as census, exit polls, etc.), marks obtained by a student in an examination, etc.

Data Item:
        A data item refers to a single unit of values. For example, roll number, name, date of birth; age, address and marks in each subject are data items. Data items can be divided in 2 types.

a. **Group Items:**–Data items that can be divided into sub-items are called Group items. For example, an address is a group item as it is divided into sub items such as house number, street number, locality, city, pin code, etc. Likewise, a date can be divided into day, month and year; a name can be divided into first name and last name.

b. **Elementary Items:**–Data items that cannot be divided into sub items are called elementary items. For example roll number, marks, city, pin code, etc. are normally treated as elementary items because they cannot be further divided.

Entity:
        Entity is something that has certain attributes or properties, which may be assigned values. For example student is an entity.

Field:
        The attributes or properties of the entity are called as field. The value assigned to these fields may be either numeric or non-numeric. For example The possible attributes for a student can be roll number, name, date of birth, gender and class. The possible values for these attributes can be 12345, VIKAS, 09/09/1985, M, 9.

Record: A record is a collection of related fields for a given entity sets.

File:
        File is a collection of related records. For example, a file containing records of all students in class, a file containing records of all employees of an organization. In fact, a file represents an entity set.

Key:
        A key is a data item in a record that takes unique values and can be used to distinguish a record from other records. It may happen that more than one data item have unique values. In that case there exists multiple keys.

But at a time, we may be using only one data item as a key, called primary key, that too depending on the problem in hand. The other key(s) are the known as alternate key(s).

In some cases, there is no field that has unique values. Then a combination of some fields can be used to form a key, such a key is known as composite key.

In worst case, if there is no possibility of forming a key from within the record, then an extra data item can be added to the record that can be used as a key.

Information:
The terms data and information have been used to mean same thing. But actually information is more than just data. In simple terms, information is a processed data. Data is just a collection of values (raw data), from which no conclusion can be drawn.

Thus data as such is not useful for decision making. When the data is processed by applying certain rules, new generated data becomes information. This new generated data (information) conveys some meaning and hence can be used for decision making.

Data Type:
A data type is a collection of values and a set of operations that act on those values. Whether our program is dealing with pre-defined data types or user-defined types, these two aspects must be considered:

A.   Set of values.
B.   Set of operations.

For example, consider an integer data type which consists of valued (MININT,...,-3, -2, -1, 0, 1, 2, 3, ..., MAXINT), where MININT and MAXINT are the smallest and largest integers that can be represented by an integer type on a particular computer.

The operations on integers include the arithmetic operation of addition (+), subtraction (-), multiplication (*), and division (/). There are also operations that test for equality/inequality and the operation that assign an integer value to a variable.

Data Types can be divided in 3 types:-

Primitive Data Type:
A primitive data type is a data type that is predefined. The predefined data type is also known as built in data type. These primitive data types may be different for different programming languages.

For example, C programming language provides built in support for integers (int, long), real's (float, double and long double) and character (char).

User defined data Type: When a primitive data type does not suits the requirement in a particular case then we can create our own types. These types are called as user defined data type.

Abstract Data Type:
ADT is a useful tool for specifying the logical properties of a data type. A data type is a collection of values and a set of operations on those values.

That collection and those operations form a mathematical construct that may be implemented using a particular hardware or software data structure. The term "abstract data type" refers to the basic mathematical concept that defines the data type.

When we define an abstract data type as a mathematical concept, we are not concerned with space or time efficiency. Those are implementation issues.

The definition of an ADT is not concerned with implementation details at all. It may not even be possible to implement a particular ADT on a particular piece of hardware or using a particular software system. ADT is a useful guideline to implementers and a useful tool to programmers who wish to use the data type correctly.

Data structure:
Data may be organized in many different ways – the logical or mathematical model organization of data is called data structures. The choice of a particular data structure depends on the following considerations.

A. It must be able to represent the relationship of the data in the real world.
B. It must be simple enough so that it can be processed efficiently as and when necessary.

The study of data structures includes:

A. Logical description of the data structure.

B. Implementation of the data structure.

C. Quantitative analysis of the data structure. This analysis includes determining the amount of memory needed to store the data structure (also called as space complexity) and the time required to process it. (also called as time complexity).

TIME COMPLEXITY:
This measure is used to estimate the running time of algorithm in terms of the size of input data. For this purpose a popular notation called big 'O' notation is used.

SPACE COMPLEXITY:

This measure is used to define extra space consumed by the algorithm except input data. This is also measured in terms of input size and big 'O' notation is also popular in this case as well.

To calculate Time and Space Complexity we use following notations:

1. **Big Oh notation:**
    The function $f(n) = O(g(n))$ (read as "f of n is big oh of g of n") if and only if there exist positive constants c and m such that $f(n) <= c*g(n)$ for all n, $n>=m$.

Example:
The function $3n+2 = O(n)$ as $3n+2 <= 4n$ for all $n>=2$.
The function $6*2^n+n^2 = O(2^n)$ as $6*2^n+n^2 <= 7*2^n$ for all $n>=4$.
We write $O(1)$ to mean a computing time that is a constant. $O(n)$ is a linear, $O(n^2)$ is called quadratic, $O(n^3)$ is called cubic, and $O(2^n)$ is called exponential. If an algorithm takes time $O(\log N)$, it is faster as compared to $O(n)$.

2. **Omega notation:-** The function $f(n) = \Omega(g(n))$ (read as "f of n is omega of g of n"). if and only if there exist positive constants c and m such that that $f(n) >= c*g(n)$ for all n, $n>=m$.

Example :
The function $3n+2 = \Omega (n)$ as $3n+2 >= 3n$ for all $n>=1$.
The function $6*2^n+n^2 = \Omega (2^n)$ as $6*2^n+n^2 >= 6*2^n$ for all $n>=1$.

3. **Theta notation:-** The function $f(n) = \Theta (g(n))$ (read as "f of n is theta of g of n"). if and only if there exist positive constants c and m such that that $c*g(n) <= f(n) <= c2*g(n)$ for all n, $n>=m$.

Example :
The function $3n+2 = \Theta (n)$ as $3n+2 >= 3n$ for all $n>=1$ and $3n+2 <= 4n$ for all $n>=2$.
The function $6*2^n+n^2 = \Theta (2^n)$.

Counting number of steps:

We can determine the number of steps needed by a program to solve a particular problem instance in one of two ways. In the first method, we introduce a new variable, count, into the program.

This is a global variable with initial value 0. Statements to increment count by the appropriate amount are introduced into the program. This is done so that each time a statement in the original program is executed, count is incremented by the step count of that statement.

```
1.                      Algorithm Sum(a, n)
2.                      {
3.                              s:= 0
4.                      count := count + 1 [count is global it is initially zero.]
5.                              for I: = 1 to n do
6.                              {
7.                                      count := count + 1  [ for FOR loop ]
8.                                      s := s + a[I]
9.                                      count := count + 1  [ for s ]
10.                             }
11.                             count := count + 1[for last time of for]
12.                             count := count + 1[for the return]
13.                             return s
14.                     }
```

Cases To Consider During Analysis-

Choosing the input to consider when analyzing an algorithm can have a significant impact on how an algorithm will perform.

For example, if the input list is already sorted, some sorting algorithms will perform very well, but other sorting algorithms may perform very poorly. The opposite may be true if the list is randomly arranged instead of sorted. Hence multiple input sets must be considered while analyzing an algorithm. These include the following

(a) **Best Case Input:**
This represents the input set that allows an algorithm to perform most quickly. With this input the algorithm takes` shortest time to execute ,as it causes the algorithms to do the least amount of work .For example ,for a searching algorithm the best case would be if the value we are searching for is found in the first location that the search algorithm checks . As a result, this algorithm would need only one comparison irrespective of the complexity of the algorithm .No matter how large is the input, searching in a best case will result in a constant time of 1 .Since the best case for an algorithm would usually be very small and frequently constant value, a best case analysis is often not done.

(b) **Worst Case Input:**
This represents the input set that allows an algorithm to perform most slowly. Worst case is an important analysis because it gives us an idea of the most time an algorithm will ever take .Worst case analysis requires that we identify the input values that cause an algorithm to do the most work .For example, for a searching algorithm, the worst case is one where the value is in the last place we check or is not in the list .This could involve comparing the key to each list value for a total of N comparisons.

(c) **Average Case Input:-**This represents the input set that allows an algorithm to deliver an average performance. Doing Average-case analysis is a four-step process. These steps are as under.

  (i) Determine the number of different groups into which all possible input sets can be divided.
  (ii) Determine the probability that the input will come from each of these groups

List of data structures:-

LINEAR DATA STRUCTURES: The elements form a sequence i.e. linear list.
  ARRAYS.
  LINK LISTS.
  STACKS.
  QUEUES.
  HASH TABLE.
NON-LINEAR DATA STRUCTURES: The elements do not form a sequence.
  1. TREES.
  2. GRAPHS.

Operation on Data Structures-

1. **Traversing:**
   To access each and every element of data structure exactly one's is called traversal of DS.

2. **Insertion:**
   To add one more data element in the data structure at a particular position is called insertion operation.

3. **Deletion:**
   To remove an element from data structure is called deletion. Deletion should be performed in such a way that remaining elements should not be in inconsistent state.

4. **Searching:**
   To find out the location of particular data element in data structure is called searching operation.

5. **Sorting:**
   To arrange all the data of data structure in a specific order is known as sorting of data.

6. **Merging:**
   To combine two data structure into a single one is called merging of data structures.

ALGORITHM:

An algorithm is a finite set of instructions that, if followed, accomplishes a task. In addition, all algorithms must satisfy following criteria:

1. Input: -   Zero or more quantities are externally supplied.
2. Output: -   At least one quantity is produced.
3. Definiteness: Each instruction is clear and unambiguous.
4. Finiteness: -   If we trace out the instructions of an algorithm, then for all cases, the algorithm terminates after a finite number of steps.
5. Effectiveness: Every instruction must be very basic so that it can be carried out, in principle, by a person using only pencil and paper.

An algorithm is a well defined list of steps for solving a particular problem. The time and spaces it uses are two major measures of the efficiency of an algorithm.

The complexity of an algorithm is the function which gives the running time or space in terms of the input size.

The formats for the presentation of an algorithm consist of two parts:

The first part is a paragraph which tells the purpose of algorithm identifies the variables which occur in algorithm and list the input data.

The second part consists of the list of steps that is to be executed.

1. set K: = 1, LOC: = 1 and MAX: = A[1] (Left to Right)

2. Comments [   ]

3. Variables in Capital Letters

4. Assignment : =

5. Comparison = , ≠

6. For input READ : Input variables

7. For Output WRITE : Output Variables

CHAPTER

∞ 2 ∞

(Introduction of Array)

Introduction-

An array is a list of a finite number of homogenous data elements. (i.e. data elements of the same type)

Arrays can be classified as:

- One-dimensional array or linear array that requires only one index to access an individual element of the array.

- Two-dimensional arrays that requires two indices to access an individual element of the array. It is also called as matrix.

- Multi-dimensional arrays for which we need two or more indices.

Linear Arrays:

An array is a list of a finite number of elements of consecutive homogenous data elements (i.e. data elements of the same type) such that:

❖ The elements of the array are referenced respectively by an index set consisting of n consecutive integer numbers.

❖

❖ The elements of the array are stored respectively in successive memory locations.

The number n of elements is called the length or size of the array. If not explicitly stated, we will assume the index set consists of the integers 1,2...n.

In general the length or the number of data elements of the array can be obtained from the index set by the formula

N = UB – LB + 1

So A is the base address (array name)
LB   is the Lower bound
UB   is the upper bound

e.g.

LB is the lower bound of array i.e. 1
Base address = 200
Find address of 3rd element Loc (A[K])

W = no. of memory cell for a single element
Loc (A[K]) = base(A) + W x (K-LB)
= 200 + 2 x (3 – 1) = 204

ADT ARRAY:

An array is a collection of homogeneous elements.

❖ We can access every element by an index number.

❖ Each element is referred with an index and the name of the array generally the index value starts with zero or one.

❖ Array is stored in memory in conjunctive locations.

Operations on Linear Arrays :-
- Traverse.
- Searching.
- Insertion.
- Deletion.
- Merging.
- Sorting.

1. Traverse:
Traversing is the process of visiting each element of the array exactly once. As the elements can be accessed directly only we have to vary an index from lower bound to upper bound in steps of one to access individual elements in order. For an array of size n, the loop executes n times so the traversal operation on linear arrays is O(n) operation.

TRAVERSE (ARR, LB, UB)
Let ARR is a linear array with lower bound LB and upper bound UB. This algorithm traverses ARR applying an operation PROCESS to each element of LA.
Step 1. Set K:=LB [Initialize counter]
Step 2. Repeat steps 3 and 4 while K <= UB
Step 3. Apply PROCESS to A[k] [Visit element.]
Step 4. Set K: = K + 1 [Increase counter] [End of Step 2]
Step 5. Exit

2. Insertion:-
To insert an element at position k first we have to move elements starting from kth position down by one position in order to accommodate the element at kth position. The best possible case occurs when the item is inserted at the last position. In this case, no element is moved down. The worst case occurs when the element is to be inserted at the first position. In this case, all the elements are moved down. Therefore loop executes n time. Thus the complexity of insertion operation is O(n) i.e. linear time.

3.INSERT (ARR, N, ITEM, POS)
Here ARR is the Linear array with N elements and POS is a positive integer such that POS <= N. This procedure insert an element ITEM at position POS in array ARR of size N
1. Set I: = N.   [Initialize I to the last element]
2. Repeat steps 3 and 4 while I >= POS:
3. Set ARR[I+1]: = ARR[I].   [Shifting elements one position down]
4. Set I: = I -1. [Decrement I by 1]   [End of step 2 loop]
5. Set ARR[POS] = ITEM.   [Inserting ITEM at POS]
6.   Set N: = N + 1.   [Reset the number N of elements in ARR]
7.   Exit.

4. Deletion:-

Deletion refers to the operation of removing an element from existing list of element. After deletion the size of the linear array is decreased by factor of one. Like insertion operation, deleting an element from the end of their linear array can be done very easily.

However, to delete an element from any other location, the elements are to be moved upward in order to fill up the location vacated by the removed element.

DELETE(ARR, N, POS)

Here ARR is the Linear array with N elements and PS is a positive integer such that POS <= N. This procedure removes an element ITEM from position POS in array ARR of size N.

1.   Set I: = POS.   [Initialize I to the element to be removed.]
2.   Repeat step 3 and 4 while I < N:
3.   Set ARR[I]: = ARR[I+1].   [Shifting elements one position up]
4.   Set I: = I + 1.   [Increment I by 1][End of step 2 loop]
5.   Set N: = N – 1.   [Reset the number N of elements in ARR]
6.   Exit.

Search Operations:-

Searching is the process of finding the location of given element in the linear array. The search is said to be successful if the given element is found i.e. the element does exist in the array, otherwise unsuccessful
There are two approaches to search operation:

1.   Linear search
2.   Binary search

Linear Search

Given no information about the array the only way to search for given element item is to compare item with each element of a one by one. This method, which traverses a sequentially to locate item is called linear search or sequential search. In the best possible case, the item may occur at first position. In this case, the search operation terminates in success with just one comparison. However the worst case occurs when either the item is present at last position or missing from the array. Thus in worst case the linear search is O(n) operations.

LINEAR_SEARCH (A, N, ITEM, LOC)

Here DATA is the Linear array with N elements and ITEM is a given item of the information. This procedure finds the locations LOC of ITEM in A or sets LOC:=0 if the search is unsuccessful.

1.	Set LOC: = 0.	[Initialize LOC]
2.	Set I: = 1.	[Initialize counter]
3.	Repeat step 4 to 6 while I <= N:	
4.	IF A[I] = ITEM ,then:	[if the item is found]
	Set LOC := I and Exit. [End of If structure]	
5.	Set I: = I + 1.	[Increment counter by 1]
	[End of step 3 loop]	
6.	Exit.	

Binary Search

This search is fast then linear search but it can be used only when array is sorted. In this searching we first find the mid of the array, if value is found at mid position then the search ends otherwise the number is searched in left half or right half.

This process is continued till the item is not found. In each iteration or in each recursive call, the search is reduced to one half of the array. Therefore, for n elements in the array, there will be $\log_2 n$ iterations or recursive call. Thus the complexity of binary search is $O(\log_2 n)$. This complexity will be same irrespective of the position of the element, even if it is not present in the array.

BINARY_SEARCH (A, N, ITEM, LOC)

Here DATA is the Linear array with N elements and ITEM is a given item of the information. This procedure finds the locations LOC of ITEM in A or sets LOC:=0 if the search is unsuccessful.

1.	Set LOW: = 1,HIGH := N.	[Initialize]
2.	Repeat step 3 to 6 while LOW <= HIGH:	
3.	Set MID := (LOW + HIGH)/2.	
4.	If A[MID] = ITEM, then:	
	Set POS := MID and Return.	
5.	Else If ITEM > A[MID], then:	
	Set LOW := MID – 1.	
6.	Else:	
	Set HIGH := MID + 1.	[End of If structure]
7.	Set POS := 0.	
8.	Exit.	

5. Merge Operation:-

       Merging is the process of combining the elements of two similar structures(linear arrays) into a single structure. Suppose that two arrays are sorted then our aim is to combine them in such a way that the combined array is also in the sorted order.

PROCEDURE MERGE(ARR1, ARR2, ARR3, N1, N2)

[This procedure merge two sorted arrays ARR1 and ARR2 into ARR3 of size N1,N2 and N1+N2 respectively.]

1.   Set I: = 1, J:=1, K:=1
2.   Repeat step 3 and 4 while I <= N1 and J <= N2
3.   If ARR1[I] < ARR2[J] , then

      (a)   Set ARR3[K]: = ARR1[I]
      (b)   Set I:= I + 1 [Increment I by 1]

      Else:

      (a)   Set ARR3[K]: = ARR2[J]
      (b)   Set J:= J + 1 [Increment J by 1] [End of If structure]

4.   Set K:=K+1 [Increment K by 1] [End of Step 2 loop]
5.   Repeat steps 6 and 7 while I <= N1 [Remaining of ARR1]
6.   Set ARR3[K]: = ARR1[I]
7.   Set K:= K+1, I:= I + 1   [End of step 5 loop]
8.   Repeat steps 9 and 10 while J <= N2 [Remaining of ARR2]
9.   Set ARR3[K]: = ARR2[J]
10.   Set K:= K+1, J:= J + 1   [End of step 8 loop]
11.   Exit.

CHAPTER
∞ 3 ∞
(Introduction of Matrix)

Introduction-

Two Dimensional Arrays (MATRIX):

A two-dimensional array is a list of finite number m*n homogeneous data element such that-

❖ The elements of array are referenced by two index set consisting of **m** and **n** consecutive integer number.

❖ The elements of the array are stored in consecutive memory location.

❖ The size of two-dimensional array is denoted by **m*n.**

Representation of Two-Dimensional Array in Memory:

Let A be a two-dimensional matrix of size m*n. Through **a** is pictured as a rectangular pattern with m row and n column.

The array will be represented in memory by a block of m*n sequential memory location. However the element can be stored in two different ways

(1) COLUMN MAJOR ORDER:

The element are stored column by column i.e. the m elements of first column are stored in first m location, element of second column are stored in next m location and so on.

(2) ROW MAJOR ORDER:

The element are stored row by row i.e. the n elements of first row are stored in first n location, element of second row are stored in next n location and so on.

The address LOC (A[J,K]) of the array can be obtain by this formula:-

Row-Major Order:

LOC(A[J, K])=Base(A)+W*[n*(J-LB)+(K-LB)]

Column-Major Order:

LOC(A[J, K])=Base(A)+W*[m*(K-LB)+(J-LB)]

Where w=no. of memory cell for a single element

An m*n matrix is a two-dimensional. Whose m, n elements are arranged in m row and n column.

A matrix is denoted by capital letters such as A,B,C......and its element are denoted by corresponding lower letters suffixed with row and column index such as a(j, k),b(j, k)......

Types of MATRIX-

Diagonal Matrix-

1	0	0	0
0	2	0	0
0	0	3	0
0	0	0	4

Tri diagonal Matrix-

1	4	0	0
2	2	4	0
0	2	3	2
0	0	3	4

Lower Triangular Matrix-

1	0	0	0
1	2	0	0
2	3	3	0
3	4	2	4

Upper Triangular Matrix-

1	3	2	1
0	2	4	2
0	0	3	3
0	0	0	4

Sparse Matrix

1	0	0	0
0	0	0	0
0	2	0	0
0	0	0	4

Dense Matrix

1	0	9	1
0	6	8	4
4	2	3	0
0	3	0	4

Unit Matrix

1	0	0	0
0	1	0	0
0	0	1	0
0	0	0	1

Symmetric Matrix

1	2	3	4
2	1	2	3
3	2	1	2
4	3	2	4

NOTE:

We assume that all the matrices (except Sparse and Dense) are square matrix.

MATRIX OPERATION-

1) Sum.
2) Multiply.
3) Transpose.
4) Sorting.

SPARSE MATRIX:

An m*n matrix is said to be sparse if many of its elements are zero. A matrix that is not sparse is called dense matrix.

Sparse matrix e.g.-diagonal matrix, tri diagonal matrix In array representation, an array of triplets of type- <row, col, element> is used to store nonzero elements where first field of the triplet is used to record row position, second to record column position and third one to record the nonzero elements of the sparse matrix. this row is header in sparse matrix.

TRANSPOSE (SM1, SM2)

Here SM1 and SM2 are two sparse matrices. This algorithm computes the transpose of SM1 into SM2. N is no. of nonzero elements. Header row is 0

1. Set MAXROW: = SM1[0,2], MAXCOL:= SM1[0,3], N:=SM1[0,1]
2. Set SM2[0,1]:= N, SM2[0,2]:=MAXCOL, SM2[0,3]:=MAXROW
3. If N>0 ,then [If number of non zero elements are more than 0]
4. Set I := 1 [I is a counter for SM2]
5. Repeat Step 6 for COL:=1 to MAXCOL [Counter for counting columns]
6. Repeat Step (a) for P:=1 to N [Counter for SM1]
    (a)   If SM1[P,3] = COL ,then
    (i) SM2[I,1]: = SM1[P,1]
    (ii) SM2[I,2]:= SM1[P,3]
    (iii) SM2[I,3]:= SM1[P,2]
    (iv) Set I := I + 1 [End of If structure.] [End of Step 6 loop]
    [End of Step 5] [End of If structure]
7. Exit.

CHAPTER
∞ **4** ∞
(SORTING)

Introduction-

Sorting means arranging a set of data in some order. There are different methods that are used to sort the data in ascending or descending order. These methods can be divided into two categories. They are as follows:-

1. **Internal Sorting:-**
    If all the data that is to be sorted can be accommodated at a time in memory then internal sorting methods are used.

2. **External Sorting:-**
    When the data to be sorted is so large that some of the data is present in the memory and some is kept in auxiliary memory (hard disk, floppy, tape, etc.), then external sorting methods are used. Merge sorting can be used in external sorting.

Internal Sorting	Best case	Average case	Worst case
1. Selection Sort	$O(N^2)$	$O(N^2)$	$O(N^2)$
2. Bubble Sort	$O(N)$	$O(N^2)$	$O(N^2)$
3. Insertion Sort	$O(N)$	$O(N^2)$	$O(N^2)$
4. Shell Sort or Diminishing Increment Sort	$O(N(\log N))^2$	$O(N(\log N))^2$	$O(N(\log N))^2$
5. Merge Sort	$O(N \log N)$	$O(N \log N)$	$O(N \log N)$
6. Radix Sort or Bucket Sort	$O(d*N)$ where d is no. of digits	$O(d*N)$ where d is no. of digits	$O(d*N)$ where d is no. of digits
7. Quick Sort or Partition Exchange Sort	$O(N \log N)$	$O(N \log N)$	$O(N^2)$
8. Heap Sort	$O(N \log N)$	$O(N \log N)$	$O(N \log N)$

1. SELECTION SORTING-

The selection sort starts from first element and searches the entire list until it finds the minimum value. The sort places the minimum value in the first place, selects the second element and searches for the second smallest element.

The process continues until the complete list is sorted. A selection sort is one in which successive elements are selected in order and placed into their proper sorted positions.

The selection process need to be done only from 1 to n-1 rather than upto n. Analysis of the selection sort is straightforward. The first pass makes n - 1 comparisons, the second pass makes n - 2 and so on. So total comparisons are $(N - 1) + (N - 2) + (N - 3) + ... + 2 + 1 = N (N-1)/2 = O (N^2)$. There is little additional storage required (except to hold a few temporary variables.).

The sort may therefore be categorized as $O(N^2)$, although it is faster than the bubble sort but there is no improvement if the input file is completely sorted or unsorted. Despite the fact that it is simple to code, it is unlikely that the straight selection sort would be used on any files but those for which n is small.

The selection sort algorithm for sorting works as follows. First find the smallest element in the list and put it in the first position. Then find the second smaller element in the list and put it in the second position.

It is to be noted that the number of comparisons in the selection sort algorithm is independent of the original sort of the elements. The selection sort method requires (n – 1) passes to sort an array.

Best case	Average case	Worst case
$O(N^2)$	$O(N^2)$	$O(N^2)$

SELECTION_SORT (A , N)

Here A is an array with N elements. This algorithm sorts the array A with N elements in ascending order.

1.   Repeat Steps 2 to 5 for I = 1 to N – 1:
2.   Set MIN: = A [I].
3.   Set POS: = I.
4.   Repeat Steps for J = I + 1 to N:
                        If A [J] < MIN, then:
                                (a) Set MIN:= A [J].
                                (b) Set POS:= J.
                        [End of If structure.]
                [End of Step 4 loop.]
5.   .   If I ≠ POS, then:
                        (a) Set TEMP: = A [I].
                        (b) Set A [I] : = A [POS].
                        (c) Set A [POS] : = TEMP.
                [End of If structure.]
        [End of step 1 loop.]
7.   Return.

2. BUBBLE SORTING-

One of the characteristics of this sort is that it is easy to understand and program. It is probably the least efficient. The basic idea underlying the bubble sort is to pass through the file sequentially several times. Each pass consists of comparing each element in the file with its successor and interchanging the two elements if they are not in proper order.

The method is called the bubble sort because each number slowly "bubbles" up to its proper position. In this sort the number of interchanges cannot be greater than the number of comparisons.

It is likely that it is the number of interchanges rather than the number of comparisons that takes up the most times in the program's execution.

The only redeeming features of the bubble sort are that it requires little additional space (one additional record to hold the temporary value for interchanging and several simple integer variables) and that it is O (N) in the case that the file is completely sorted (or most completely sorted).

This follows from the observation that only one pass of (N–1) comparisons (and no interchanges) is necessary to establish that a sorted file is sorted. Bubble sort technique posses one very important property:-

" Once there is no swapping of elements in a particular pass, there will be no further swapping of elements in the subsequent passes. " This property can be exploited to reduce the unnecessary (redundant) passes.

For this purpose we can use a flag to determine if any interchange has taken place, if yes only then proceed with the next pass; otherwise stop. The first pass makes n - 1 comparisons , the second pass makes n – 2 and so on. So total comparisons are (N - 1)+ (N - 2) + (N - 3) + ... + 2 + 1 = N (N-1)/2 = $O(N^2)$.

Best case	Average case	Worst case
O (N)	O (N^2)	O (N^2)

BUBBLE_SORT (A , N)

Here A is an array with N elements. This algorithm sorts the array A with N elements in ascending order.

1.   Set SWAP: = True.
2.   Set I: = 1.
3.   Repeat Steps 4 to 6 while I < N AND SWAP = True:
4.   Set SWAP : = False.
5.   Repeat Steps for J:= 1 to N – I:
                        If A [J] > A [J + 1] , then:
                                (a) Set TEMP:= A [J].
                                (b) Set A [J]:= A [J +1].
                                        (c) Set A [J + 1]:= TEMP.
                                (d) Set SWAP:= True.
                        [End of If structure.]
                [End of Step 5 loop.]
6.   Set I : = I + 1.
        [End of Step 3 loop.]
7.   Return.

3.INSERTION SORTING-

An insertion sort is one that sorts a set of records by inserting records into an existing sorted file. If the initial file is sorted only one comparisons is made on each pass, so that the sort is O(N). If the file is initially sorted in the reverse order, the sort is O(N²).

The simple insertion sort is still usually better than the bubble sort. The closer the file is to be sorted order, the more efficient the simple insertion sort becomes. The average number of comparisons in the simple insertion sort (by considering all possible permutations of the input array) is also O(n²).

The space requirements for the sort consist of only one temporary variable. Both the selection sort and the simple insertion sort are more efficient than bubble sort. Selection sort requires fewer assignments than insertion sort but more comparisons.

The insertion sort algorithm is a very slow algorithm when n is very large. Insertion sort is usually used only when n in small. This algorithm is very popular with bridge players when they first sort their cards. In this procedure, we pick up a particular value and then insert it at the appropriate place in the sorted sub list.

The worst case performance occurs when the elements of the input array are in descending order. The first pass makes 1 comparison , the second pass makes 2 and last pass makes N-1 comparisons. So total comparisons are $1 + 2 .... + (N - 2) + (N - 1) = N(N-1)/2 = O(N^2)$.

Best case	Average case	Worst case
O (N)	O (N²)	O (N²)

INSERTION_SORT (A , N).
Here A is an array with N elements. This algorithm sorts the array A with N elements in ascending order.
1.   Repeat Steps 2 to 5 for I = 2 to N:
2.   Set ITEM: = A [I].
3   Set J : = I – 1.
4.   Repeat Steps while J >= 1 AND A[J] > ITEM:
                        (a)   Set A[J+1]:=A[J]. [Moves element forward.]
                        (b)   Set J:= J - 1.
                [End of Step 4 loop.]
5.   Set A [J+1]:= ITEM.   [Inserts element in proper place.]
        [End of Step 1 loop.]
6.   Return.

4. SHELL SORTING-

It is also called as **diminishing increment sort**, named after its discoverer. Shell sort algorithm provides more significant improvement on simple insertion sort. This method sorts separate sub files of the original file. These sub files contain every kth element of the original file. The value of k is called an increment or a gap.

The idea behind the shell sort is a simple one. We have already noted that the simple insertion sort is highly efficient on a file that is in almost sorted order. It is also important to realize that when the file size n is small an $O(N^2)$ sort is often more efficient than an $O(N \log N)$ sort.

The reason for this is that $O(N^2)$ sorts are generally quite simple to program and involve very few actions other than comparisons and replacements on each pass. An $O(N \log N)$ sort is generally quite complex and employs a large number of extra operations on each pass in order to reduce the work of subsequent passes. When n is larger $(N \log N)$. is better than (N^2). However when n is small (N^2) is not much larger than $(N \log N)$, so that a large difference in those constants often causes an $O(N^2)$ sort to be faster.

Since the first increment used by the shell sort is large the individual sub files are quite small so that the simple insertion sorts on those sub files are fairly fast. Each sort of a sub file causes the entire file to be more nearly sorted.

Thus, although successive passes of the shell sort use smaller increments and therefore deal with larger sub files those sub files are almost sorted due to the actions of previous passes. Thus, the insertion sorts on those sub files are also quite efficient.

In this connection it is significant to note that if a file is partially sorted using an increment k and is subsequently partially sorted using an increment j, the file remains partially sorted on the increment k. That is subsequent partial sorts do not disturb earlier ones.

The actual time requirements for a specific sort depend on the number of elements in the array increments and on their actual values. When span equals to 1 the array is almost sorted. It has been shown that the order of the shell sort can be approximated by $O\ (n(\log n)^2)$ if an appropriate sequence of increments is used. In general the shell sort is recommended for files having several hundred elements.

Best case	Average case	Worst case
$O\ (N(\log N)^2\ )$	$O\ (N(\log N)^2\ )$	$O\ (N(\log N)^2\ )$

SHELL_SORT (A , N)

Here A is an array with N elements. This algorithm sorts the array A with N elements in ascending order.

1.   Set SPAN:= N / 2.   [Initializes]
2   Repeat Steps from 3 to 5 while SPAN >= 1:
3.   Set I:= SPAN + 1.
4.   Repeat Steps while I <= N:
                          (a) Set ITEM := A[I].
                          (b) Set J := I – SPAN.
                          (c) Repeat Steps while J>=1 AND A[J]>ITEM:

(i)   Set A [J + SPAN]:= A[J].   [Shifting.]
(ii)   Set J:= J - SPAN.
                          [End of Step (c) loop.]
                    (d) Set A[J+SPAN] := ITEM. [Insert.]
                    (e) Set I:= I + 1. [End of Step 4 loop.]

5.   Set SPAN:= SPAN / 2. [End of Step 2 loop.]
6.   Return.

5. MERGE SORTING-

Merging means combining two sorted lists into one sorted list. For this the elements from both the sorted lists are compared. The smaller of both the elements is then stored in the third array.

Merge Sort is a sorting algorithm that uses the idea of divide and conquers. This algorithm divides the array into smaller files, sorts them separately and then merges them. The major work is done in the merge procedure, which is an O(N) operation. The only disadvantage of merge sort is that it uses an extra temporary array of the same size as that of input array to merge the two arrays.

The elements of the temporary array are copied back to the original array before the next merging. In merge sort the splitting is simple but the joining is hard (merging the two sorted files).

In quick sort the splitting is hard (partitioning) and the joining is simple (the two halves and the pivot automatically form a sorted array).

Best case	Average case	Worst case
O (N log N)	O (N log N)	O (N log N)

MERGE_SORT (A , N)

Here A is an array with N elements. This algorithm sorts the array A with N elements in ascending order.

1.   Set SIZE:= 1.
2.   Repeat Steps 3 to 7 While SIZE < N:
3.   Set L1:= 1 , K:= 1.
4.   Repeat Steps While (L1 + SIZE) <= N:

          (a)   Set L2:= L1 + SIZE.
          (b)   Set U1:= L2 - 1.
          (c)   If U1 + SIZE <= N, then:
                      Set U2 := U1 + SIZE.
          (d)   Else:
                      Set U2 := N .   [End of if structure.]
          (e)   Repeat Steps For I:= L1 to U1 and J:= L2 to U2:
                      If A [I] < A [J], then:
                        (i) Set TEMP [K]:= A [I].
                        (ii) Set I:= I + 1.
                      Else:
                        (i) Set TEMP [K]:= A [J].
                        (ii) Set J:= J + 1. [End of if structure.]
                      Set K:= K + 1.
              [End of Step (e) loop.]
          (f)   Repeat Steps While I <= U1:
                      (i)   Set TEMP [K]:= A [I].
                      (ii)   Set K:= K + 1.
                      (iii)   Set I:= I + 1.
              [End of Step (f) loop.]
          (g)   Repeat Steps While J <= U2:
                      (i)   Set TEMP [K]:= A [J].
                      (ii)   Set K:= K + 1.
                      (iii)   Set J:= J + 1.
              [End of Step (g) loop.]
          (h)   Set L1:= U2 + 1.
        [End of Step 4 loop.]
5.   Repeat Steps While L1 <= N:
               (i)   Set TEMP [L1]:= A [L1].
               (ii)   Set L1:= L1 + 1.
          [End of Step 5 loop.]
6.   Repeat Steps For I:= 1 to N:
               (i)   Set A [I]:= TEMP [I].
               (ii)   Set I:= I + 1.
          [End of Step 6 loop.]
7.   Set SIZE:= SIZE * 2.
        [End of Step 2 loop.]
8.   Return.

6. RADIX SORTING-

A radix sort also called Bucket sort is the method used by most of the people when sorting a list of names in alphabetic order. The procedure we follows is: (a) First the names are grouped according to the first letter, thus the names are arranged in 26 classes, one for each letter of the alphabet.

First class consists of those names that begin with letter A, the second class consists of those names that begin with letter B, and so on. (b) Next, the names are grouped according to the second letter.

After this step, the list of names will be sorted on first two letters. (c) This process is continued for the number of times depending on the length of the names with maximum letters.

If shorter names, we assume those names padded with blanks. Since there are 26 letters of the alphabet, we make use of 26 buckets, one for each letter of the alphabet. After grouping these names according to their specific letter, we collect them in order of buckets i.e. first we pick up names from first bucket (for letter A), then from second bucket (for letter B), and so on.

This new list becomes input for next pass i.e. to separate them on the next letter from left. To sort decimal numbers, where radix or base is 10, we need ten buckets. These buckets are numbered 0,1,2,3,4,5,6,7,8,9. Unlike sorting names decimal numbers are sorted from right to left i.e. first on unit digit, then on tens digit, then on hundredth digit, and so on.

The above process is to be repeated for the number of times depending on the number of digits in the largest number.

The smaller numbers are treated as filled with leading zeroes and they will go to bucket numbered 0. And secondly the number appearing in the bottom of the bucket has smaller index, and while collecting the numbers it is collected first.

Thus from above discussion we conclude that bucket sort performs well only when the number of digits in the elements are very small.

Best case	Average case	Worst case
O (d *N) where d is no. of digits	O (d *N) where d is no. of digits	O (d *N) where d is no. of digits

MAX (A , N , MAXITEM)

Here A is an array with N elements. This algorithm finds the maximum of N elements in A and assigns it to MAXITEM.
1.   Set MAXITEM:= 0.
2.   Repeat Steps 3 and 4 For I:= 1 to N:
3.   If A [I] > MAXITEM , then:
                        Set MAX:= A [I].
                [End of if structure.]
4.   Set I:= I + 1.
        [End of Step 2 loop.]
5.   Return.

DIGIT_COUNT (MAXITEM , COUNT)

1.   Set COUNT:= 0.
2.   Repeat Steps 3 and 4 While MAXITEM ≠ 0:
3.   Set MAXITEM:= INT(MAXITEM / 10).
4.   Set COUNT = COUNT + 1.
        [End of Step 2 loop.]
5.   Return

DIGIT (N , I , DIG)

1.   Set DIG:= 0.
2.   Repeat Steps 3 and 4 For J := 1 to I:
3.   Set DIG := N MOD 10.
4.   Set N:= N / 10.
        [End of Step 2 loop.]
    4. Return.

RADIX_SORT (A , N)

Here A is an array with N elements. This algorithm sorts the array A with N elements in ascending order. We have assumed that first index of array is 0

1.   [Calling of MAX Function.]
        Call MAX (A , N, MAXITEM).
2.   [Calling of DIGIT_COUNT Function.]
        Call DIGIT_COUNT(MAXITEM, D).
3.   Repeat Steps 4 to 7 For K : = 1 to D:
                [Initialize MAT array with ∞]
4.   Repeat Steps For I: = 0 to 9:
                        (a) Repeat Steps For J: =0 to N-1:
                                Set MAT [I] [J]:= ∞.
                        [End of Step (a) loop.]

[End of Step 4 loop.]
5. Repeat Steps For I:= 0 to N-1:
    (a) [Calling of DIGIT Function.]
         Call DIGIT (A [I] , K, ROW).
    (b) Set COL := 0.
    (c) Repeat Steps While MAT [ROW] [COL] $\neq \infty$:
             Set COL:= COL + 1.
         [End of Step (c) loop.]
    (d) Set MAT[ROW][COL]:= A [I].
    (e) Set I:= I + 1.
    [End of Step 5 loop.]
6. Set L:= 0.
7. Repeat Steps For I: = 0 to 9:
    (a) Repeat Steps For J: = 0 to N-1:
             If MAT [I] [J] $\neq \infty$, then:
                 (i) Set A [L] = MAT [I] [J].
                 (ii) Set L:= L + 1.
             [End of if structure.]
         [End of Step (a) loop.]
    [End of Step 7 loop.]
    [End of Step 3 loop.]
8. Return.

7. QUICK SORTING-

Quick Sort is a algorithm that also like merge sort uses the idea of divide and conquer. This algorithm finds the element that divides (splits) the array into halves in such a way that the elements in the left sub array are less than and the elements in the right sub array are greater than the dividing (splitting) element.

Then these two-sub arrays are sorted separately. This procedure is recursive. The main task in quick sort is to find the element that divides the array into halves and to place it at its proper location in the array. Usually the procedure places the first element in the array at its final position.

To find the location of the element that splits the array into two sections is an O (N) operation, because every element in the array is compared to the dividing element.

After the division each section is examined separately. If the array is split approximately in half (which is not usually), then there will be log2n splits.

Quick sort is sensitive to the order of the input data and it gives the worst-case performance when the elements are already in the ascending or descending order.

Then it divides the array into sections of 1 and n-1 elements in each call. Thus, there will be n-1 divisions in all. The efficiency of quick sort is affected by the initial order of elements.

This sort is also called as partition exchange sort. The quick sort has the property that it works best for files that are "completely unsorted" and worst for files that are completely sorted. The situation is precisely the opposite for the bubble sort, which works best for sorted files and worst for unsorted files.

It is possible to speed up quick sort for sorted files by choosing a random element of each sub-file as the pivot value. If a file is known to be nearly sorted this might be a good strategy (although in that case choosing the middle element as a pivot would be even better).

However if nothing is known about the file such a strategy does not improve the worst case behavior since it is possible (although improbable) that the random element chosen each time might consistently be the smallest element of each sub-file. As a practical matter sorted files are more common than a good random number generator happening to choose the smallest element repeatedly.

The analysis for the case in which the file size is not an integral power of 2 is similar but slightly more complex the results however remain the same. It can be shown however that on the average (over all files of size n) the quick sort makes approximately 1.386n Log2n comparisons even in its unmodified version.

In practical situations quick sort is often the fastest available because of its low overhead and its average O(N log N) behavior. The space requirements for the quick sort depend on the number of nested recursion calls or on the size of the stack.

The reason for this is that a smaller sub-array will be divided fewer times than a larger sub-array. Of course, the larger sub-array will ultimate be processed and subdivided but this will occur after the smaller sub-arrays have already been sorted and therefore removed from the stack.

Another advantage of quick sort is locality of reference. That is over a short period of time all array accesses are to one or two relatively small portions of the array (a sub-file or portion thereof).

This ensures efficiency in the virtual memory environment where pages of data are constantly being swapped back and forth between external and internal storage. Locality of reference results in fewer page swaps being required for a particular program A simulation study has shown that in such an environment quick sort uses less space-time resources than any other sort considered.

The efficiency can be improved by:
1. Choosing a better pivot element.
2. Using better algorithm for small sub – lists.
3. Eliminating recursion.

Best case	Average case	Worst case
O (N log N)	O (N log N)	O (N²)

QUICKSORT (A , LB , UB)

Here A is an array with LB lower bound and UB upper bound. This algorithm sorts the A array in ascending order.
1.   Set MID:= 0.
2.   If LB >= UB, then Return.
3.   [Calling of Partition Function].
        Call PARTITION (A , LB , UB, MID).
4.   [Calling of Quick sort Function].
        Call QUICKSORT (A , LB , MID - 1).
5.   [Calling of Quick sort Function].
        Call QUICKSORT (A , MID + 1 , UB).
6.   Return.

PARTITION (A , LB , UB, MID)

Here A is an array with LB lower bound and UB upper bound. This algorithm assigns the mid value of the total elements in the array in the MID.

1.   Set DOWN:= LB.
2.   Set UP:= UB.
3.   Set PIVOT:= A [DOWN].
4.   Repeat Steps 5 to 9 While DOWN < UP:
5.   Repeat Step (a) While A[DOWN] <=PIVOT AND DOWN < UB:
                (a)   Set DOWN:= DOWN + 1.
            [End of Step 5 loop.]
6.   Repeat Step (a) While A [UP] > PIVOT:
                (a)   Set UP:= UP - 1.
            [End of Step 6 loop.]

7.   If DOWN < UP, then:
            (a)   Set TEMP:= A [DOWN].
            (b)   Set A [DOWN]:= A [UP].
            (c)   Set A [UP]:= TEMP.
        [End of If Structure.]
        [End of Step 4 loop.]
8.   Set A [LB]:= A [UP].
9.   Set A [UP] := PIVOT
10.   Set MID = UP.
11.   Exit.

8. HEAP SORTING-

In this method a tree structure called heap is used. A heap is a type of a binary tree. An ordered balanced binary tree is called a min heap where the value at the root of any sub-tree is less than or equal to the value of either of its children.

An ordered balanced binary tree is called a max-heap when the value at the root of any sub-tree is more than or equal to the value of either of its children. It is not necessary that the two children must be in some order. Sometimes the value in left child may be more than the value at right child and some other times it may be the other way round.

Heap sort is basically an improvement over the binary tree sort. It does not create nodes as in case of binary tree sort. Instead it builds a heap by adjusting the position of elements within the array itself.

Basically there are tow phases involved in sorting the elements using heap sort algorithm. They are as follows:

1. Construct a heap by adjusting the array elements.
2. Repeatedly eliminate the root element of the heap by shifting it to the end of the array and then restore the heap structure with remaining elements.

The heap sort is, therefore an O(N log N).
To analyze the heap sort note that a complete binary tree with n nodes (where n is one less than a power of two) has log(n+1) levels. Thus if each element in the array were a leaf requiring it to be filtered through the entire tree both while creating and adjusting the heap the sort would still be O(N log N).

In the average case the heap sort is not as efficient as the quick sort. Experiments indicate that heap sort requires twice as much time as quick sort in the worst case. In fact **heap sort remains O(N log N) in the worst case.**

Heap sort is also **not very efficient for small n** because of the overhead of initial heap creation and computation of the location of fathers and sons. The space requirements for the heap sort (aside from array indices) is only one additional record to hold the temporary for switching provided the array implementation of an almost complete binary tree is used.

Best case	Average case	Worst case
O (N log N)	O (N log N)	O (N log N)

INSHEAP(TREE, N, ITEM)

A heap H with N elements is stored in the array TREE, and an ITEM of information is given.

This procedure inserts ITEM as a new element of H. PTR gives the location of ITEM as it rises in the tree, and PAR denotes the location of the parent of ITEM.

1.   [Add new node to H and initialize PTR.]
        Set N: = N + 1 and PTR := N.
2.   [Find location to insert ITEM.]
        Repeat Steps 3 to 6 while PTR > 1:
3   Set PAR := [PTR / 2] . [Location of parent node.]
4   If ITEM <= TREE[PAR], Then:
                        Set TREE[PTR] := ITEM, and Return.
                [End of If Structure]
5   Set TREE[PTR]:= TREE[PAR]. [Moves node down.]
6.   Set PTR := PAR. [Updates PTR.]
        [End of Step 2 loop.]
7.   [Assign ITEM as the root of H.]
        Set TREE[1] := ITEM.
8.   Return.

DELHEAP (TREE, N, ITEM)

A heap H with N elements is stored in the array TREE. This procedure assigns the root TREE [1] of H to the variable ITEM and then reheaps the remaining elements.

The variable LAST saves the value of the original last node of H. The pointer PTR, LEFT and RIGHT give the locations of LAST and its left and right children as LAST sinks in the tree.

1. Set ITEM: = TREE [1]. [Removes last node of H.]
2. Set LAST: = TREE [N] and N: = N-1. [Removes last node of H.]
3. Set PTR: = 1, LEFT: = 2 and RIGHT: = 3 [Initialize pointers.]
4. Repeat Steps 5 to 7 while RIGHT ≤ N:
5.   If LAST ≥ TREE [LEFT] and LAST ≥ TREE [RIGHT], then:
        Set TREE [PTR]: = LAST and Return.
    [End of If structure.]
6.   If TREE [RIGHT] ≤ TREE [LEFT], then:
        Set TREE [PTR]: = TREE [LEFT] and PTR: = LEFT.
    Else:
        Set TREE [PTR]: = TREE [RIGHT] and PTR: = RIGHT.
    [End of If structure.]
7.   Set LEFT: = 2 * PTR and RIGHT: = LEFT + 1.
    [End of Step 4 loop.]
8. If LEFT = N and LAST < TREE [LEFT], then:
    Set TREE[PTR]:= TREE[LEFT], PTR: = LEFT.
    [End of If structure.]
9. Set TREE [PTR]: = LAST.
10. Return.

HEAPSORT(A, N)

An array A with N elements is given. This algorithm sorts the elements of A.
1. [Build a heap H]
    Repeat For J:= 1 To N-1:
        Call INSHEAP (A, J, A[J+1]).
    [End of loop.]
2. [Sort A by repeatedly deleting the root of H,]
    Repeat while N > 1:
        (a)   Call DELHEAP (A, N, ITEM).
        (b)   Set A[N+1]:=ITEM.
    [End of Loop.]
3. Exit.

C Programs-

1. Selection sorting (First Logic)

```
1.      #include<stdio.h>
2.      #include<conio.h>
3.      #define SIZE 10
4.      void selection_sort(int [], int);
5.      void main()
6.      {
7.              int a[SIZE],i,n;
8.              clrscr();
9.              printf("Enter how many elements");
10.             scanf("%d",&n);
11.             /*Input Array*/
12.             for(i=0;i<n;i++)
13.             {
14.                     printf("Enter element %d ",i+1);
15.                     scanf("%d",&a[i]);
16.             }
17.             selection_sort(a,n);
18.             /* Output Array*/
19.             for(i=0;i<n;i++)
20.                     printf("%d ",a[i]);
21.             getch();
22.      }
23.      void selection_sort(int a[], int n)
24.      {
25.             int i,j,t,min,minpos;
26.             for(i=0;i<n-1;i++)
27.             {
28.                     min = a[i];
29.                     minpos = i;
30.                     for(j=i+1;j<n;j++)
31.                     {
32.                             if(a[j] < min)
33.                             {
34.                                     min = a[j];
35.                                     minpos = j;
36.                             }
37.                     }
38.                     if(i != minpos)
39.                     {
40.                             t = a[i];
41.                             a[i] = a[minpos];
42.                             a[minpos] = t;
43.                     } } }
```

2. Selection sorting (Second Logic)

```
1.      #include<stdio.h>
2.      #include<conio.h>
3.      #define SIZE 10
4.      void selection_sort(int [], int);
5.      void main()
6.      {
7.              int a[SIZE],n,i;
8.              clrscr();
9.              printf("Enter how many elements ");
10.             scanf("%d", &n);
11.             /*Input array*/
12.             for(i=0;i<n;i++)
13.             {
14.                     printf("Enter element %d ",i+1);
15.                     scanf("%d", &a[i]);
16.             }
17.             selection_sort(a,n);
18.             /*Output array*/
19.             for(i=0;i<n;i++)
20.                     printf("%d ",a[i]);
21.             getch();
22.     }
23.     void selection_sort(int a[],int n)
24.     {
25.             int minpos ;
26.             int i,j,t;
27.             for(i=0;i<n-1;i++)
28.             {
29.                     minpos = i ;
30.                     for(j=i+1;j<n;j++)
31.                     {
32.                             if(a[minpos] > a[j])
33.                                     minpos = j ;
34.                     }
35.                     if( minpos != i)
36.                     {
37.                             t = a[i];
38.                             a[i] = a[minpos];
39.                             a[minpos] = t;
40.                     }
41.             }
42.     }
```

3. Bubble sorting .

```c
1.      #include<stdio.h>
2.      #include<conio.h>
3.      #define SIZE 10
4.      void bubble_sort(int [],int);
5.      void main()
6.      {
7.              int a[SIZE],n,i;
8.              printf("Enter how many elements");
9.              scanf("%d",&n);
10.             /*Input Array*/
11.             for(i=0;i<n;i++)
12.             {
13.                     printf("Enter element %d ",i+1);
14.                     scanf("%d",&a[i]);
15.             }
16.             bubble_sort(a,n);
17.             /*Output Array*/
18.             for(i=0;i<n;i++)
19.                     printf("%d ",a[i]);
20.             getch();
21.     }
22.     void bubble_sort(int a[],int n)
23.     {
24.             int i,j,swap,t;
25.             swap=1;
26.             i=1;
27.             while(i<n && swap == 1)
28.             {
29.                     swap = 0;
30.                     for(j=0;j<n-i;j++)
31.                     {
32.                             if(a[j]>a[j+1])
33.                             {
34.                                     t = a[j];
35.                                     a[j]=a[j+1];
36.                                     a[j+1] = t;
37.                                     swap = 1;
38.                             }
39.                     }
40.                     i++;
41.             }
42.     }
```

4. Insertion sorting -

```
1.      #include<stdio.h>
2.      #include<conio.h>
3.      #define SIZE 10
4.      void insertion_sort(int [], int);
5.      void main()
6.      {
7.              int a[SIZE],i,n;
8.              clrscr();
9.              printf("Enter how many elements");
10.             scanf("%d",&n);
11.             /*Input Array*/
12.             for(i=0;i<n;i++)
13.             {
14.                     printf("Enter element %d ",i+1);
15.                     scanf("%d",&a[i]);
16.             }
17.             insertion_sort(a,n);
18.             /* Output Array*/
19.             for(i=0;i<n;i++)
20.             printf("%d ",a[i]);
21.             getch();
22.     }
23.     void insertion_sort(int a[], int n)
24.     {
25.             int i,j,item;
26.             for(i=1;i<n;i++)
27.             {
28.                     item = a[i];
29.                     /*shifting*/
30.                     for(j=i-1;j>=0 && a[j] >item ;j--)
31.                             a[j+1] = a[j];
32.                     /*insert*/
33.                     a[j+1] = item;
34.             }
35.     }
```

5.. Shell sorting –

```
1.      #include<stdio.h>
2.      #include<conio.h>
3.      #define SIZE 10
4.      void shell_sort(int [], int);
5.      void main()
6.      {
7.              int a[SIZE],i,n;
8.              clrscr();
9.              printf("Enter how many elements");
10.             scanf("%d",&n);
11.             /*Input Array*/
12.             for(i=0;i<n;i++)
13.             {
14.                     printf("Enter element %d ",i+1);
15.                     scanf("%d",&a[i]);
16.             }
17.             shell_sort(a,n);
18.             /* Output Array*/
19.             for(i=0;i<n;i++)
20.                     printf("%d\n",a[i]);
21.             getch();
22.     }
23.     void shell_sort(int a[], int n)
24.     {
25.             int i,j,item,span;
26.             span = n/2;
27.             while(span >= 1)
28.             {
29.                     for(i=span;i<n;i++)
30.                     {
31.                             item = a[i];
32.                             /*shifting*/
33.                             for(j=i-span;j>=0 && a[j] >item ;j-=span)
34.                                     a[j+span] = a[j];
35.                             /*insert*/
36.                             a[j+span] = item;
37.                     }
38.                     span = span /2;
39.             }
40.     }
```

6. . Radix sorting -

```
1.      #include<stdio.h>
2.      #include<conio.h>
3.      #define SIZE 10
4.      void radix_sort(int [], int);
5.      int max(int [],int);
6.      int cnt_digit(int);
7.      int digit(int,int);
8.      void main()
9.      {
10.             int a[SIZE],n,i;
11.             clrscr();
12.             printf("enter how many elements");
13.             scanf("%d",&n);
14.             /*Input Array*/
15.             for(i=0;i<n;i++)
16.             {
17.                     printf("enter element %d ",i+1);
18.                     scanf("%d",&a[i]);
19.             }
20.             radix_sort(a,n);
21.             /*Output Array*/
22.             for(i=0;i<n;i++)
23.                     printf("%d\n",a[i]);
24.             getch();
25.     }
26.     void radix_sort(int a[],int n)
27.     {
28.             int mat[10][SIZE],i,j,k,l,row,col,m,d;
29.             m = max(a,n);
30.             d = cnt_digit(m);
31.             for(k=1;k<=d;k++)
32.             {
33.                     /*initialize matrix with sentinel value -1*/
34.                     for(i=0;i<10;i++)
35.                             for(j=0;j<n;j++)
36.                                     mat[i][j] = -1;
37.                     /*copy array A to matrix mat*/
38.                     for(i=0;i<n;i++)
39.                     {
40.                             row = digit(a[i],k);
41.                             col = 0;
42.                             while(mat[row][col] != -1)
43.                                     col++;
```

```
44.                              mat[row][col] = a[i];
45.                          }
46.                          /*copy matrix to array except sentinel value -1*/
47.                          l=0;
48.                          for(i=0;i<10;i++)
49.                                  for(j=0;j<n;j++)
50.                                          if(mat[i][j] != -1)
51.                                                  a[l++] = mat[i][j];
52.                  }
53.          }
54.          int max(int a[],int n)
55.          {
56.                  int m,i;
57.                  m = a[0];
58.                  for(i=1;i<n;i++)
59.                  {
60.                          if(a[i] > m)
61.                                  m = a[i];
62.                  }
63.                  return (m);
64.          }
65.          int cnt_digit(int n)
66.          {
67.                  int c=0;
68.                  while(n>0)
69.                  {
70.                          c++;
71.                          n = n / 10;
72.                  }
73.                  return (c);
74.          }
75.          int digit(int n, int k)
76.          {
77.                  int a,i=1;
78.                  while(i<= k)
79.                  {
80.                          a = n % 10;
81.                          n = n / 10;
82.                          i++;
83.                  }
84.                  return (a);
85.          }
```

7. Merge sorting (Non Recursive)

```
1.      #include<stdio.h>
2.      #include<conio.h>
3.      #define SIZE 10
4.      void merge_sort(int [], int );
5.      void main()
6.      {
7.              int a[SIZE],n,i;
8.              clrscr();
9.              printf("Enter how many elements");
10.             scanf("%d",&n);
11.             /* Input Array */
12.             for(i=0;i<n;i++)
13.             {
14.                     printf("enter element %d ",i+1);
15.                     scanf("%d",&a[i]);
16.             }
17.             merge_sort(a,n);
18.             /*Output Array*/
19.             for(i=0;i<n;i++)
20.                     printf("%d\n",a[i]);
21.             getch();
22.     }
23.     void merge_sort(int a[],int n)
24.     {
25.             int i,j,k,lb1,lb2,ub1,ub2,t[SIZE],sz;
26.             sz = 1;
27.             while(sz<n)
28.             {
29.                     lb1 = 0;
30.                     k = 0;
31.                     while((lb1+sz)<n)
32.                     {
33.                             lb2 = lb1+sz;
34.                             ub1 = lb2-1;
35.                             ub2 = (ub1+sz)<n ? (ub1+sz) : n-1;
36.                             /*merging*/
37.                             for(i=lb1,j=lb2; i<=ub1 && j <= ub2; k++)
38.                             {
39.                                     if(a[i] < a[j])
40.                                             t[k] = a[i++];
41.                                     else
42.                                             t[k] = a[j++];
43.                             }
44.                             /*remaining of 1st file*/
```

```
45.                          while(i<=ub1)
46.                              t[k++] = a[i++];
47.                          /*remaining of 2nd file*/
48.                          while(j<=ub2)
49.                              t[k++] = a[j++];
50.                          lb1 = ub2 + 1;
51.                      }
52.                      /*copy any rem. file not in pair*/
53.                      while(k<n)
54.                      {
55.                          t[k] = a[k];
56.                          k++;
57.                      }
58.                      /* copy t array into a*/
59.                      for(i=0;i<n;i++)
60.                          a[i] = t[i];
61.                      sz = 2*sz;
62.                  }
63.      }
```

9. Merge sorting (Recursive)

```
1.       #include<stdio.h>
2.       #include<conio.h>
3.       #define SIZE 10
4.       void merging(int [], int ,int ,int , int);
5.       void mergesort(int [],int , int );
6.       void main()
7.       {
8.               int a[SIZE],i,n;
9.               printf("Enter how many elements");
10.              scanf("%d",&n);
11.              /*Input Array*/
12.              for(i=0;i<n;i++)
13.              {
14.                      printf("enter element %d ",i+1);
15.                      scanf("%d",&a[i]);
16.              }
17.              mergesort(a,0,n-1);
18.              /*Output Array*/
19.              for(i=0;i<n;i++)
20.                      printf("%d ",a[i]);
21.              getch();
22.      }
23.      void merging(int a[], int l1,int u1,int l2, int u2)
```

```
24.     {
25.            int i,j,k,t[SIZE];
26.            for(i=l1,j=l2,k=l1;i<=u1 && j <= u2;k++)
27.            {
28.                    if(a[i]<a[j])
29.                            t[k]=a[i++];
30.                    else
31.                            t[k]=a[j++];
32.            }
33.            /*Remaining of first file*/
34.            while(i<=u1)
35.                    t[k++] = a[i++];
36.            /*Remaining of second file*/
37.            while(j<=u2)
38.                    t[k++] = a[j++];
39.            for(i=l1;i<=u2;i++)
40.                    a[i] = t[i];
41.     }
42.     void mergesort(int a[],int lb, int ub)
43.     {
44.            int mid;
45.            if(lb<ub)
46.            {
47.                    mid = (lb+ub)/2;
48.                    mergesort(a,lb,mid);
49.                    mergesort(a,mid+1,ub);
50.                    merging(a,lb,mid,mid+1,ub);
51.            }
52.     }
```

10. Quick Sorting (Recursive)

```
1.      #include<stdio.h>
2.      #include<conio.h>
3.      #define SIZE 10
4.      int partition(int [], int, int);
5.      void quick_sort(int [], int, int);
6.      void main()
7.      {
8.             int a[SIZE],n,i;
9.             clrscr();
10.            printf("Enter how many elements");
11.            scanf("%d",&n);
12.            /*Input Array*/
13.            for(i=0;i<n;i++)
```

```c
14.                     {
15.                             printf("Enter element %d ",i+1);
16.                             scanf("%d",&a[i]);
17.                     }
18.             quick_sort(a,0,n-1);
19.             /*Output Array*/
20.             for(i=0;i<n;i++)
21.                     printf("%d\n",a[i]);
22.             getch();
23.     }
24.     int partition(int a[], int lb,int ub)
25.     {
26.             int down,up,t,pivot;
27.             down = lb;
28.             up = ub;
29.             pivot = a[lb];
30.             while(down < up)
31.             {
32.                     while(a[down] <= pivot && down < up)
33.                             down++;
34.                     while(a[up] > pivot)
35.                             up--;
36.                     if(down < up)
37.                     {
38.                             t = a[down];
39.                             a[down] = a[up];
40.                             a[up] = t;
41.                     }
42.             }
43.             a[lb] = a[up];
44.             a[up] = pivot;
45.             return (up);
46.     }
47.     void quick_sort(int a[], int lb, int ub)
48.     {
49.             int mid;
50.             if(lb >= ub)
51.                     return;
52.             mid = partition(a,lb,ub);
53.             quick_sort(a,lb,mid-1);
54.             quick_sort(a,mid+1,ub);
55.     }
```

11. Quick sorting (Non-Recursive)

```
1.      #include<stdio.h>
2.      #include<conio.h>
3.      #define SIZE 10
4.      #define MAXSTK 20
5.      struct stack
6.      {
7.              int data[MAXSTK];
8.              int top;
9.      };
10.     void push(struct stack *,int );
11.     int pop(struct stack *);
12.     int isfull(struct stack);
13.     int isempty(struct stack);
14.     void quick_sort(int [],int);
15.     int partition(int a[],int,int);
16.     void main()
17.     {
18.             int a[SIZE],n,i;
19.             clrscr();
20.             printf("Enter how many elements ");
21.             scanf("%d",&n);
22.
23.             /*Input Array*/
24.             for(i=0;i<n;i++)
25.             {
26.                     printf("Enter element %d ",i+1);
27.                     scanf("%d",&a[i]);
28.             }
29.             quick_sort(a,n);
30.             /*Output Array*/
31.             for(i=0;i<n;i++)
32.                     printf("%d ",a[i]);
33.             getch();
34.     }
35.     void quick_sort(int a[],int n)
36.     {
37.             struct stack stklb,stkub;
38.             int mid = 0,lb,ub;
39.             lb = 0;
40.             ub = n-1;
41.             stklb.top = -1;
42.             stkub.top = -1;
43.             if(n>1)
44.             {
```

```
45.                      push(&stklb,lb);
46.                      push(&stkub,ub);
47.            }
48.        while(!isempty(stklb))
49.        {
50.                lb = pop(&stklb);
51.                ub = pop(&stkub);
52.                mid=partition(a , lb , ub );
53.                if(lb<mid-1)
54.                {
55.                        push(&stklb,lb);
56.                        push(&stkub,mid-1);
57.                }
58.                if(mid+1<ub)
59.                {
60.                        push(&stklb,mid+1);
61.                        push(&stkub,ub);
62.                }
63.            }
64.    }
65.    int partition(int a[],int lb,int ub)
66.    {
67.            int t = 0,up = 0,down = 0,temp = 0;
68.            down = lb;
69.            up = ub;
70.            temp = a[down];
71.            while(down < up)
72.              {
73.                        while( (a[down] <= temp ) && ( down < up )
)
74.                            down++;
75.                        while( a[up] > temp)
76.                            up--;
77.                        if(down < up)
78.                         {
79.                                t = a[down];
80.                                a[down] = a[up];
81.                                a[up] = t;
82.                         }
83.                }
84.            a[lb] = a[up];
85.            a[up]= temp;
86.            return(up);
87.    }
88.    void push(struct stack *p,int val)
89.    {
```

```
90.            if(isfull(*p))
91.              {
92.                   printf("Stack is Full.");
93.                   return;
94.              }
95.            p->top++;
96.            p->data[p->top]=val;
97.    }
98.    int pop(struct stack *p)
99.    {
100.           int val;
101.           if(isempty(*p))
102.             {
103.                  printf("Stack is Empty.");
104.                  return NULL;
105.             }
106.           val=p->data[p->top];
107.           p->top--;
108.           return(val);
109.   }
110.   int isfull(struct stack p)
111.   {
112.           return(p.top==MAXSTK-1);
113.   }
114.   int isempty(struct stack p)
115.   {
116.           return(p.top==-1);
117.   }
```

12. Quick sorting (Using median as pivot)

```
1.     #include<stdio.h>
2.     #include<conio.h>
3.     #define SIZE 10
4.     void quick_sort(int [],int,int);
5.     int partition(int a[],int,int);
6.     void main()
7.     {
8.             int a[SIZE],n,i;
9.             clrscr();
10.            printf("Enter how many elements ");
11.            scanf("%d",&n);
12.            /*Input Array*/
13.            for(i=0;i<n;i++)
14.            {
15.                    printf("Enter element %d ",i+1);
```

```
16.                            scanf("%d",&a[i]);
17.                    }
18.             quick_sort(a,0,n-1);
19.             /*Output Array*/
20.             for(i=0;i<n;i++)
21.                     printf("%d ",a[i]);
22.             getch();
23.     }
24.     void quick_sort(int a[],int lb,int ub)
25.     {
26.             int mid = 0;
27.             if(lb>=ub)
28.              return;
29.             mid=partition(a , lb , ub );
30.             quick_sort(a , lb , mid-1 );
31.             quick_sort(a , mid+1 , ub);
32.     }
33.     int partition(int a[],int lb,int ub)
34.     {
35.             int t = 0,up = 0,down = 0,temp = 0,pos;
36.             down = lb;
37.             up = ub;
38.             /* This function returns
39.                     1 if median is found at lb
40.                     2 if median is found at (lb+ub)/2
41.                     3 if median is found at ub        */
42.             pos=median(a[down],a[(down + up)/2],a[up]);
43.             /*Swap the median with element stored at lb*/
44.             if(pos == 2)
45.             {
46.                     t = a[lb];
47.                     a[lb]=a[(lb+ub)/2];
48.                     a[(lb+ub)/2] = t;
49.             }
50.             else if(pos == 3)
51.             {
52.                     t = a[lb];
53.                     a[lb] = a[ub];
54.                     a[ub] = t;
55.             }
56.             temp = a[lb];
57.             while(down < up)
58.                {
59.                             while( (a[down] <= temp ) && ( down < up )
)
60.                                     down++;
```

```
61.                              while( a[up] > temp)
62.                                    up--;
63.                              if(down < up)
64.                              {
65.                                    t = a[down];
66.                                    a[down] = a[up];
67.                                    a[up] = t;
68.                              }
69.                      }
70.              a[lb] = a[up];
71.              a[up]= temp;
72.              return(up);
73.      }
74.      int median(int a, int b, int c)
75.      {
76.              if(a>b && b>c || c>b && b>a)
77.                      return 2;
78.              if(b>a && a>c || c>a && a>b)
79.                      return 1;
80.              if(a>c && c>b || b>c && c>a)
81.                      return 3;
82.              return 0;
83.      }
```

13. Heap sorting -

```
1.       #include<stdio.h>
2.       #include<conio.h>
3.       #define SIZE 10
4.       void insheap(int [], int, int);
5.       int delheap(int [], int);
6.       void heapsort(int [], int);
7.       void main()
8.       {
9.              int a[SIZE],i,n;
10.             clrscr();
11.             printf("Enter how many elements");
12.             scanf("%d",&n);
13.             /*Input Array*/
14.             for(i=0;i<n;i++)
15.             {
16.                     printf("Enter element %d ",i+1);
17.                     scanf("%d",&a[i]);
18.             }
19.             heapsort(a,n);
20.
```

```
21.              /*Output Array*/
22.              for(i=0;i<n;i++)
23.                      printf("%d ",a[i]);
24.              getch();
25.      }
26.      void insheap(int tree[], int n, int item)
27.      {
28.              int ptr,par;
29.              n++;
30.              ptr=n;
31.              while(ptr>0)
32.              {
33.                      par = (ptr-1)/2;
34.                      if(item<= tree[par])
35.                      {
36.                              tree[ptr]=item;
37.                              return;
38.                      }
39.                      tree[ptr]=tree[par];
40.                      ptr = par;
41.              }
42.              tree[0] = item;
43.      }
44.      int delheap(int tree[],int n)
45.      {
46.              int item,ptr,last,left,right;
47.              item = tree[0];
48.              last = tree[n];
49.              ptr = 0;
50.              left = 1;
51.              right = 2;
52.              while(right<=n)
53.              {
54.                      if(last>= tree[left] && last>= tree[right])
55.                      {
56.                              tree[ptr] = last;
57.                              return(item);
58.                      }
59.                      if(tree[right]<= tree[left])
60.                      {
61.                              tree[ptr]=tree[left];
62.                              ptr=left;
63.                      }
64.                      else
65.                      {
66.                              tree[ptr]=tree[right];
```

```
67.                              ptr=right;
68.                      }
69.                      left = 2*ptr+1;
70.                      right = left+1;
71.              }
72.              if(left == n-1 && last < tree[left])
73.              {
74.                      tree[ptr] = tree[left];
75.                      ptr = left;
76.              }
77.              tree[ptr] = last;
78.              return(item);
79.      }
80.      void heapsort(int a[], int n)
81.      {
82.              int item,j;
83.              for(j= 0; j<n-1; j++)
84.                      insheap(a,j,a[j+1]);
85.              while(n>0)
86.              {
87.                      item=delheap(a,n-1);
88.                      a[n-1] = item;
89.                      n--;
90.              }
91.      }
```

CHAPTER
∞ 5 ∞
(STACK)

Introduction-

A stack is one of the most commonly used data structure. A stack also called a Last-In-First-Out (LIFO) system is a linear list in which insertions and deletions can take place only at one end called the top. The insertion and deletion operations in stack terminology are known as push and pop operations.

Definition:

A stack is an ordered collection of items into which new items may be inserted and from which items may be deleted at one end called the top of the stack.

The above definition specifies that a single end of the stack is designated as the stack top. New items may be put on top of the stack (In this case the top of the stack moves upward to correspond to the new highest element), or items which are at the top of the stack may be removed (In which case the top of the stack moves downward to correspond to the new highest element).

We must decide which end of the stack is designated as its top i.e., at which end items are added or deleted. The two changes which can be made to a stack are given special names. When an item is added to a stack it is pushed onto the stack and when an item is removed it is popped from the stack. Because of the push operation which adds elements to a stack, a stack is sometimes called a **pushdown list.**

There is no upper limit on the number of items that may be kept since the definition does not specify how many items are allowed in the collection. Pushing another item onto a stack merely produces a larger collection of items.

However if a stack contains a single item and the stack is popped the resulting stack contains no items and is called the empty stack. Although the push operation is applicable to any stack the pop operation cannot be applied to the empty stack because such a stack has no elements to pop.

Therefore, before applying the pop operator to a stack we must ensure that the stack is not empty. The operation isempty(s1) determines whether or not a stack s1 is empty. If the stack is empty, isempty(s1) returns the value TRUE otherwise it returns the value FALSE.

Like the operation pop, peek is not defined for an empty stack. The result of an illegal attempt to pop or access an item from an empty stack is called underflow. Underflow can be avoided by ensuring that isempty(s1) is false before attempting the operation pop(s1) or the peek(s1).

Use of Stack:
In general a stack can be used in any situation that calls for a (LIFO) last-in, first-out discipline or that displays a nesting pattern.

Implementation of Stack:
Stack can be implemented by using either array or by using linklist.

1. Representing a stack using an array:

To implement a stack we need a variable, called top that holds the index of the top element of the stack and an array to hold the elements of the stack. Let us suppose that the elements of the stack are of integer type and the stack can store maximum of 10 such elements i.e. stack size is 10.

We have defined our own data type named stack, which is structure and whose first element top will be used as an index to the top element and an array elements of size MAXSIZE whose elements are of integer type to hold the elements of the stack. At the last we declare variable s1 of type stack. With these declarations we will write develop functions for variable operation to be performed on the stack.

Limitation:-

The array based representation of stacks suffers from following limitations:

1. Size of the stack must be known in advance.

2. We may come across situations when an attempt to push an element causes overflow. However stack as an abstract data structure can not be full. Hence, abstractly it is always possible to push an element onto stack. Therefore representing stack as an array prohibits the growth of stack beyond the finite number of elements.

2. Representing a stack using a linked list:

A stack represented using a linked list is also known as **linked stack.** We have defined our own data type named stack, which is a self-referential structure and whose first element info hold the element of the stack and the second element next holds the address of the element under it in the stack. At the last we declare a pointer variable top of type stack.

Creating an empty stack:-Before we can use a stack it is to be initialized. To initialize a stack we will create a empty linked list. The empty linked list is created by setting pointer variable top to value NULL.

Push operation:-To push a new element onto the stack the element is inserted in the beginning of the linked list.

Pop operation:-To pop an element from the stack the element is removed from the beginning of the linked list.

Testing stack for underflow:-The stack is tested for underflow condition by checking whether the linked list is empty. The empty status of the linked list will be indicated by the NULL value of pointer variable top.

Testing stack for overflow:-Since a stack representing using a linked list can be grow to a limit of a computer's memory there overflow condition never occurs. Hence this operations is not implemented for linked stacks.

Dispose a stack:-Because stack is implemented using linked lists therefore it is programmers job to write the code to release the memory occupied by the stack.

This dispose operations is O(n) time.

Operations on stacks:

The following operations are performed on stacks.

1. Creating an empty stack.
2. PUSH (STACK, ITEM) - to push element ITEM onto stack STACK.
3. POP (STACK) - to access and remove the top element of the stack STACK.
4. PEEK (STACK) - to access the top element of the stack STACK without removing the top element from the stack. Also called as **PEEP**.

ADT STACK:

A stack of elements of type T is a finite sequence of elements of T together with the operations

1. Initialize the stack to be empty.
2. Determine if the stack is empty or not.
3. Determine if the stack is full or not.
4. If the stack is not full, insert a new node at one end of the stack, called its top.
5. If the stack is not empty, then retrieve the node at its top.
6. If the stack is not empty delete the node at its top.

Creating an empty stack:

Before we can use a stack it is to be initialized. As the index of array elements can take any value in the range 1 to MAXSTACK the purpose of initializing the stack is served by assigning value 0 (sentinel value) to the top variable.

Push operation:

Before the push operation if the stack is full then the value of the top will be equals to MAXSTACK and then push operation can't be performed. If the stack is not full then the value of the top will be the index of the element currently on the top. Therefore before we place value onto the stack the value of the top is incremented so that it points to the new top of stack, where incoming element is placed.

Pop operation:

Before the pop operation if the stack is empty then the value of the top will be equals to 0(sentinel value) and then pop operation can't be performed. The element on the top of stack is assigned to a local variable, which later on will be returned. After assigning the top element to a local variable the variable top is decremented so that it points to the new top.

Testing stack for underflow:

Before we remove an item from a stack it is necessary to test whether stack will have some elements i.e. to test that whether the stack is empty or not. If it is not empty then the pop operation can be performed to remove the top element. This test is performed by comparing the value of top with sentinel value 0.

Testing stack for overflow:

Before we insert new item onto stack it is necessary to test whether stack still have some space to accommodate the incoming element i.e. to test that whether the stack is fill or not. If it is not full then the push operation can be performed to insert the element at top of the stack. This test is performed by comparing the value of the top with value MAXSTACK, the largest index value that the top can take.

Accessing top element (PEEK):

There may be instances where we want to access the top element of the stack without removing it from the stack (i.e. without poping it).

Efficiency:

All of these operation runs in **O(1)** time.

Application of stack:

Stack is a most commonly used data structure. Some of its applications are:

1. Stacks are used to pass parameters between functions. On a call to a function, the parameters and local variables are put on a stack.

2. High level programming languages, such as Pascal, C, etc., that provides support for recursion use stack for bookkeeping. Remember, in each recursive call there is need to save the current values of parameters local variables and the return address (the address where the control has to return the call).

3. Parenthesis checker is a program that checks whether a mathematical expression is properly parenthesized. We will consider three sets of grouping symbols: the standard parenthesis "()", braces "{}", and brackets "[]".

4. For an input expression it verifies that for each left parenthesis, brace, or bracket, there is a corresponding closing symbol and the the symbols are appropriately nested.

Mathematical Notation Translation:

First of all we will consider various types of notations for writing mathematical expressions. There are following set of operations:-

Symbol Used		Operation	Performed Precedence
**********		******************	*********
^	(Exponention)	Power	Highest
*	(Asterisk)	Multiplication	Next Highest
/	(Slash)	Division	Next Highest
+	(Plus)	Addition	Lowest
-	(Hyphen)	Subtraction	Lowest

Note1: In some cases we also use a symbol $, ** or ↑ as a power of a number.

Note2: For simplicity we will assume that a given expression contains no unary operation. We also assume that the operations on the same level of precedence are performed from left to right except ^ which works from right to left.

POLISH Notation:

1. Infix Notation:

In this notation the operator symbol is placed between its two operands. For example to add A to B we can write as A + B, to subtract D form C we write as C - D

2. Polish (Prefix) Notation:

In this notation named after the polish mathematician **Jan Lukasiewicz** the operator symbol is placed before its two operands. For example, to add A to B we can write as +AB or +BA, to subtract D from C we have to write as -CD not as –DC

In order to translate an arithmetic expression in infix notation to polish notation, we do step by step using brackets ([ ]) to indicate the partial translation.

The fundamental property of polish notation is that the order in which the operations are to perform is completely determined by the positions of the operators and operands in the expression.

Accordingly one never needs parentheses when writing expressions in polish notation. This notation is also called prefix notation.

3. Reverse Polish (Postfix) Notation:

In this notation the operator symbol is placed its two operands. For example, to add A to B we can write as AB+ or BA+, to subtract D from C we have to write as CD- not as DC-

In order to translate an arithmetic expression in infix notation to reverse polish notation we do step by step using brackets ([ ]) to indicate the partial translation.

Like polish notation here too one never needs the use of parentheses when writing expressions in polish notation. This notation is frequently called **postfix** (or **suffix**) notation.

Usage of stack in procedure call for saving return address:

Stacks are frequently used to indicate the order of the procedure calls. Suppose that while processing some procedure A if we are required to move on to procedure B, whose completion is required in order to complete procedure A. Then we place the procedure A in the STACK and begin procedure B.

However, suppose that while processing B we are led to procedure C, for some reason. Then we place B on the STACK above, and begin process C. Now if we are able to complete procedure C then we may continue to procedure B, which is on the top of the STACK.

Hence we remove the procedure B from the STACK and begin procedure B. Now when we complete procedure B then we remove procedure A from the STACK leaving STACK as empty. Finally after completing procedure A we stop.

At each stage of the above processing, the stack automatically maintaining the order that is required to complete the processing.

Now Lets disscuss some important Algorithms.

1. **PUSH (STACK, TOP, MAXSTK, ITEM)**

   This procedure adds a new ITEM at the TOP of a stack.
   1. [Stack already filled?]
      If TOP = MAXSTK, then: Write: OVERFLOW, and Return.
   2. Set TOP:= TOP + 1.   [Increases TOP by 1.]
   3. Set STACK [TOP]: = ITEM. [Inserts ITEM in new TOP position.]
   4. Return .

2. **POP (STACK, TOP, ITEM)**

   This procedure removes the TOP element of STACK and assigns it to the variable ITEM.

   1. [Stack has an item to be removed?]
      If TOP = 0, then: Write: UNDERFLOW, and Return.
   2. Set ITEM:= STACK[TOP].   [Assigns TOP element to ITEM.]
   3. Set TOP:=TOP - 1.   [Decreases TOP by 1.]
   4. Return.

3. **PEEK (STACK, TOP, ITEM)**

   This procedure shows the top element of STACK without removing it and assigns it to the variable ITEM.

   1. [Stack has an item to be showed?]
      If TOP = 0, then: Write: UNDERFLOW, and Return.
   2. Set ITEM:= STACK[TOP].   [Assigns TOP element to ITEM.]
   3. Return.

4. **INTOPOST (Q, P)**

   Suppose Q is an arithmetic expression written in infix notation. This algorithm finds the equivalent postfix expression P.
   1. Push "(" onto STACK, and add ")" to the end of Q.
   2. Scan Q from left to right and repeat steps 3 to 6 for each element of Q until the STACK is empty:
   3. If an operand is encountered, add it to P.
   4. If an left parenthesis is encountered, push it onto STACK.
   5. If an operator $\otimes$ is encountered, then:
      (a) Repeatedly pop from STACK and add to P each operator (on the top of STACK) which has the same precedence as or higher precedence then $\otimes$.

(b) Add $\otimes$ to STACK.
[End of If structure.]

6.   If a right parenthesis is encountered, then:
(a) Repeatedly pop from STACK and add to P each operator (on the top of STACK) until a left parenthesis is encountered.

(b) Remove the left parenthesis.
        [Do not add the left parenthesis to P.]
[End of If structure.]
[End of Step 2 loop.]

7.   Exit.

5.   INTOPRE (Q, P)

Suppose Q is an arithmetic expression written in infix notation. This algorithm finds the equivalent prefix expression P.

1.   Push ")" onto STACK, and add "(" to the beg of Q.
2.   Scan Q from right to left and repeat steps 3 to 6 for each element of Q until the STACK is empty:
3.   If an operand is encountered, add it to P.
4.   If an right parenthesis is encountered, push it onto STACK.
5.   If an operator $\otimes$ is encountered, then:
(a) Repeatedly pop from STACK and add to P each operator (on the top of STACK) which has the higher precedence then $\otimes$.
(b) Add $\otimes$ to STACK.
[End of If structure.]

6.   If a left parenthesis is encountered, then:
(a) Repeatedly pop from STACK and add to P each operator (on the top of STACK) until a right parenthesis is encountered.

(b) Remove the right parenthesis. [Do not add the right parenthesis to P.]
[End of If structure.]
    [End of Step 2 loop.]

7.   Reverse P.
8.   Exit.

6.   EVALPOST (P, VALUE)
This algorithm finds the VALUE of an arithmetic expression P written in postfix notation.

1.   Add a right parenthesis ")" at the end of P. [This acts as a sentinel.]
2.   Scan P from left to right and Repeat Steps 3 and 4 for each element of P until the sentinel ")" is encountered.
3.   If an operand is encountered, put it on STACK.

4.   If an operator ⊗ is encountered, then:
                (a) Remove the two top elements of STACK, where A is the
                      top   element and B is the next-to-top element.

                (b) Evaluate B ⊗ A.
                (c) Place the result of (b) back on STACK.
            [End of If structure.]
            [End of Step 2 loop.]
5.   Set VALUE equal to the top element on STACK.
6.   Exit

7.   EVALPRE (P, VALUE)

This algorithm finds the VALUE of an arithmetic expression P written in prefix notation.
1.   Add a left parenthesis "(" at the beg of P. [This acts as a sentinel.]
2.   Scan P from right to left and Repeat Steps 3 and 4 for each element of P until the sentinel "(" is encountered.
3.   If an operand is encountered, put it on STACK.
4.   If an operator ⊗ is encountered, then:
                (a) Remove the two top elements of STACK, where A is the
                top element and B is the next-to-top element.

                (b) Evaluate A ⊗ B.
                (c) Place the result of (b) back on STACK.
            [End of If structure.] [End of Step 2 loop.]
5.   Set VALUE equal to the top element on STACK.
6.   Exit

8.   PARENTHESIS_MATCHING (EQ, VALID)

This algorithm checks whether the expression EQ written in infix notation is valid or not and assigns TRUE or FALSE to VALID.

1. Scan EQ from left to right until end of equation is encountered:
2.   If "(" is encountered then: put it in the STACK.
3.   If closing bracket is encountered then:
                (a) If STACK is empty, then Set VALID:= FALSE and return.
                (b) Pop the "(" from the STACK.
            [End of If structure.] [End of Step 2 loop.]
4. If STACK is empty, then:
          Set VALID := TRUE.
7. Else:
          Set VALID := FALSE
    [End of If structure.]
8. Return

9.   TOWER (N, BEG, AUX, END)

This procedure gives a recursive solution to the Towers of Hanoi problem for N disks.
1.   If N = 1, then:
        (a)   Write: BEG → END.
        (b)   Return.
[End of If structure.]

2.   [Move N – 1 disks from BEG to AUX.]
        Call TOWER(N – 1, BEG,END,AUX).

3.   Write: BEG → END.

4.   [Move N – 1 disks from AUX to END.]
        Call TOWER(N – 1, AUX, BEG, END).

5.   Return

10.   TOWER (N, BEG, AUX, END)

This is a non-recursive solution to the Tower of Hanoi problem for N disks which is obtained by translating the recursive solution. Stacks STN, STSRC, STTARG, STAUX and STADD will correspond respectively, to the variables N, BEG, AUX, END and ADD.

0.   Set TOP:= NULL [Initially all stacks are empty]
1.   If N = 1, then:
        (a)   Write: BEG → END.
        (b)   Go to Step 5
    [End of If structure]
2.   [Translation of "Call TOWER(N-1, BEG, END, AUX)"]
        [Push current values and new return address onto stacks.]
            (i)   Set TOP: = TOP + 1
            (ii)   Set STN[TOP]: = N, STBEG[TOP]: = BEG
                    STEND[TOP]: = END, STAUX[TOP]: = AUX,
                    STADD[TOP]: = 3
        [Reset Parameters.]
            Set N: = N – 1, BEG: = BEG, AUX: = END, END: = AUX
        (C)   Go to Step 1
3.   Write: BEG → END.
4.   [Translation of "Call TOWER(N-1, AUX, BEG, END)"]
        (a)   [Push current values and new return address onto stacks.]
            (i)   Set TOP: = TOP + 1
            (ii)   Set STN[TOP]: = N, STBEG[TOP]: = BEG,

STEND[TOP]: = END, STAUX[TOP]: = AUX,
STADD[TOP]: = 5

    (b)   [Reset Parameters.]
Set N: = N – 1, BEG:= AUX, AUX: = BEG,
END = END

Go to Step 1

5.   [Translation of "Return"]
    (a)   If TOP: = NULL, then Return.
    (b)   [Restore top values on stacks.]
        (i)   Set N: = STN[TOP], BEG: = STBEG[TOP],
END: = STEND[TOP], AUX: = STAUX[TOP],
ADD: = STADD[TOP]
        (ii)   Set TOP: = TOP – 1
    (c)   Go to Step ADD

11.   QUICK (A, N, BEG, END, LOC)

Here A is an array with N elements. Parameters BEG and END contain the boundary values of the sub list of A to which this procedure applies. LOC keeps track of the position of the first element. A[BEG] of the sub list during the procedure. The local variables LEFT and RIGHT will contain the boundary values of the list of elements that have not been scanned.

1.   [Initialize.] Set LEFT:=BEG, RIGHT:=END and LOC:=BEG.
2.   [Scan from right to left.]
    (a)   Repeat while A[LOC] <= A[RIGHT] and LOC ≠ RIGHT:
        RIGHT:=RIGHT-1.
    [End of loop.]
    (b)   If LOC = RIGHT, then: Return.
    (c)   If A[LOC] > A[RIGHT], then:
        (i) [Interchange A[LOC] and A[Right].]
TEMP:= A[LOC], A[LOC]:=A[RIGHT], A[RIGHT]:=
TEMP.
        (ii)   Set LOC:= RIGHT.
        (iii)   Go to Step 3.
    [End of If structure.]
3.   [Scan from left to right.]
    (a)   Repeat while A[LEFT] <= A[LOC] and LEFT ≠ LOC:
        LEFT:=LEFT +1.
    [End of loop.]
    (b)   If LOC = LEFT, then: Return.
    (c)   If A[LEFT] > A[LOC] then
        (i) [Interchange A[LOC] and A[Left].]

TEMP:=   A[LOC],   A[LOC]:=A[LEFT],
A[LEFT]:= TEMP.
(ii)   Set LOC:= LEFT.
(iii)   Go to Step 2.
[End of If structure.]

(Quicksort) This algorithm sorts an array A with N elements.

1.   [Initialize.] Set TOP := NULL.
2.   [Push boundary values of A onto stacks when A has 2 or more elements.]
      If N > 1, then: TOP:= TOP + 1, LOWER[1]:= 1, UPPER[1]:=N.
3.   Repeat Steps 4 to 7 while TOP ≠ NULL:
4.   [Pop sublist from stacks.]
          Set BEG:= LOWER[TOP], END:= UPPER[TOP], TOP:=TOP-1.
5.   Call QUICK(A, N, BEG,END, LOC).
6.   [Push left sublist onto stacks when it has 2 or more elements.]
          If BEG < LOC – 1, then:
              TOP:=TOP+1,   LOWER[TOP]:=BEG,
          UPPER[TOP]:=LOC-1.
          [End of If structure.]
7.   [Push right sublist onto stacks when it has 2 or more elements.]
          If LOC + 1 < END, then:
              TOP:=TOP+1,LOWER[TOP]:=LOC+1,UPPER[TOP]:=
          END.
          [End of If structure.]
      [End of Step 3 loop.]
8.   Exit.

1.   Stack Operations:-

```
1.    #include<stdio.h>
2.    #include<conio.h>
3.    #define MAXSTK 10
4.    struct stack
5.    {
6.            int data[MAXSTK];
7.            int top;
8.    };
9.    void push(struct stack *,int );
10.   int pop(struct stack *);
11.   int peep(struct stack);
12.   void main()
13.   {
14.           int ch,item;
15.           struct stack s1;
16.           s1.top = -1;
17.           do
18.           {
19.                   clrscr();
20.                   printf("\t\t\tMAIN MENU\n");
21.                   printf("\t\t\t********\n\n");
22.                   printf("\t\t 1. Push in a Stack.\n");
23.                   printf("\t\t 2. Pop from the Stack.\n");
24.                   printf("\t\t 3. Stack Top or Peep.\n");
25.                   printf("\t\t 4. Exit.\n\n");
26.                   printf("\t\t Enter your choice:- ");
27.                   scanf("%d",&ch);
28.                   clrscr();
29.                   switch(ch)
30.                   {
31.                       case 1:
32.                   printf("Enter the value which is to be Push:- ");
33.                           scanf("%d",&item);
34.                           push(&s1,item);
35.                           break;
36.                       case 2:
37.                           item=pop(&s1);
38.                           printf("Pop Value==> %d",item);
39.                           break;
40.                       case 3:
41.                           item=peep(s1);
42.                   printf("Stack Top Value==> %d",item);
```

```
43.                                  break;
44.                        case 4:
45.                                  break;
46.                     default:
47.                                  printf("Wrong Choice !.Try Again
.");
48.                 }
49.            getch();
50.        }while(ch!=4);
51.    }
52.    void push(struct stack *p,int item)
53.    {
54.            if(p->top == MAXSTK-1)
55.            {
56.                    printf("Overflow.");
57.                    return;
58.            }
59.            p->top++;
60.            p->data[p->top]=item;
61.    }
62.
63.    int pop(struct stack *p)
64.    {
65.            int item;
66.            if(p->top == -1)
67.            {
68.                    printf("Underflow");
69.                    return NULL;
70.            }
71.            item=p->data[p->top];
72.            p->top--;
73.            return(item);
74.    }
75.    int peep(struct stack s1)
76.    {
77.            int item;
78.            if(s1.top == -1)
79.            {
80.                    printf("Stack is Empty.");
81.                    return(NULL);
82.            }
83.            item=s1.data[s1.top];
84.            return(item);
85.    }
```

2.   Infix to Postfix and Prefix Equation:-

```
1.      #define MAXSTK 10
2.      #include<stdio.h>
3.      #include<conio.h>
4.      #include<string.h>
5.      struct stack
6.      {
7.              int top;
8.              char data[MAXSTK];
9.      };
10.     void push(struct stack *, char );
11.     char pop(struct stack *);
12.     char peep(struct stack);
13.     int isoperator(char);
14.     int preced(char);
15.     void intopost(char [], char []);
16.     void intopre(char [],char []);
17.     void main()
18.     {
19.             char in[50],post[50],pre[50];
20.             clrscr();
21.             printf("Enter equation in infix form enclosed in brackets");
22.             gets(in);
23.             intopost(in,post);
24.             intopre(in,pre);
25.     printf("Eq. in post form is %s\nEq in pre form is %s",post,pre);
26.             getch();
27.     }
28.     void push(struct stack *p , char item)
29.     {
30.             if(p->top==MAXSTK-1)
31.             {
32.                     printf("Overflow");
33.                     return;
34.             }
35.             p->top++;
36.             p->data[p->top] = item;
37.     }
38.     char pop(struct stack *p)
39.     {
40.             char item;
41.             if(p->top == -1)
42.             {
43.                     printf("Underflow");
44.                     return (NULL);
```

```c
45.                 }
46.                 item = p->data[p->top];
47.                 p->top--;
48.                 return (item);
49.       }
50.       char peep(struct stack s1)
51.       {
52.                 char item;
53.                 if(s1.top == -1)
54.                 {
55.                         printf("Underflow");
56.                         return (NULL);
57.                 }
58.                 item = s1.data[s1.top];
59.                 return (item);
60.       }
61.       int isoperator(char ch)
62.       {
63.                 if(ch == '+' || ch == '-' || ch == '*' || ch == '/' || ch == '%')
64.                         return (1);
65.                 else
66.                         return (0);
67.       }
68.       int preced(char op)
69.       {
70.                 switch(op)
71.                 {
72.                         case '+':
73.                         case '-':
74.                                 return (1);
75.                         case '*':
76.                         case '/':
77.                                 return (2);
78.                         default :
79.                                 return (0);
80.                 }
81.       }
82.       void intopost(char in[], char post[])
83.       {
84.                 struct stack s1;
85.                 int i,j;
86.                 char ch;
87.                 s1.top = -1;
88.                 i = j = 0;
89.                 while(in[i] != '\0')
90.                 {
```

```
91.                        if(in[i] == '(')
92.                                push(&s1,in[i]);
93.                        else if(in[i] == ')')
94.                        {
95.                                ch = pop(&s1);
96.                                while(ch != '(')
97.                                {
98.                                        post[j++] = ch;
99.                                        ch = pop(&s1);
100.                               }
101.                       }
102.                   else if(isoperator(in[i]))
103.                       {
104.                               ch = peep(s1);
105.                   while(ch != '(' && preced(ch)>=preced(in[i]))
106.                       {
107.                               post[j++] = pop(&s1);
108.                               ch = peep(s1);
109.                       }
110.                       push(&s1,in[i]);
111.                   }
112.                   else
113.                           post[j++] = in[i];
114.                   i++;
115.               }
116.           post[j] = '\0';
117.   }
118.   void intopre(char in[], char pre[])
119.   {
120.           struct stack s1;
121.           int i,j;
122.           char ch;
123.           s1.top = -1;
124.           i = j = 0;
125.           while(in[i] != '\0')
126.                   i++;
127.           i--;
128.           while(i>= 0)
129.           {
130.                   if(  in[i] == ')' )
131.                           push(&s1,in[i]);
132.                   else if(in[i] == '(')
133.                   {
134.                           ch = pop(&s1);
135.                           while(ch != ')')
136.                           {
```

```
137.                              pre[j++] = ch;
138.                              ch = pop(&s1);
139.                         }
140.                    }
141.               else if(isoperator(in[i]))
142.               {
143.                    ch = peep(s1);
144.                    while(ch != ')' && preced(ch)>preced(in[i]))
145.                    {
146.                         pre[j++] = pop(&s1);
147.                         ch = peep(s1);
148.                    }
149.                    push(&s1,in[i]);
150.               }
151.               else
152.                    pre[j++] = in[i];
153.               i--;
154.          }
155.     pre[j] = '\0';
156.     strrev(pre);
157. }
```

3.   Evaluate a Postfix and Prefix equation:-

```
1.   #define MAXSTK 10
2.   struct stack
3.   {
4.        int top;
5.        int data[MAXSTK];
6.   };
7.   void push(struct stack *, int );
8.   int pop(struct stack *);
9.   int isoperator(char);
10.  int evalpost(char []);
11.  int evalpre(char []);
12.  int eval(char, int, int);
13.  void main()
14.  {
15.       char post[50],pre[50];
16.       int ans;
17.       clrscr();
18.       printf("Enter string in postfix form");
19.       gets(post);
20.       ans = evalpost(post);
21.       printf("Result of post eq is %d\n",ans);
22.       printf("Enter string in prefix form");
```

```c
23.              gets(pre);
24.              ans = evalpre(pre);
25.              printf("Result of pre eq is %d\n",ans);
26.              getch();
27.      }
28.      void push(struct stack *p , int item)
29.      {
30.              if(p->top == MAXSTK-1)
31.              {
32.                      printf("Overflow");
33.                      exit(0);
34.              }
35.              p->top++;
36.              p->data[p->top] = item;
37.      }
38.      int pop(struct stack *p)
39.      {
40.              int item;
41.              if(p->top == -1)
42.              {
43.                      printf("Underflow");
44.                      exit(0);
45.              }
46.              item = p->data[p->top];
47.              p->top--;
48.              return (item);
49.      }
50.      int isoperator(char ch)
51.      {
52.              if(ch == '+' || ch == '-' || ch == '*' || ch == '/' || ch == '%')
53.                      return (1);
54.              else
55.                      return (0);
56.      }
57.      int eval(char op, int op1, int op2)
58.      {
59.              switch(op)
60.              {
61.                      case '+': return (op1+op2);
62.                      case '-': return (op1-op2);
63.                      case '*': return (op1*op2);
64.                      case '/': return (op1/op2);
65.                      default:  return (0);
66.              } }
68.      int evalpost(char post[])
69.      {
```

```
70.              struct stack s1;
71.              int i,a,b,ans;
72.              s1.top = -1;
73.              i = 0;
74.              while(post[i] != '\0')
75.              {
76.                      if(isoperator(post[i]))
77.                      {
78.                              b = pop(&s1);
79.                              a = pop(&s1);
80.                              ans = eval(post[i],a,b);
81.                              push(&s1,ans);
82.                      }
83.                      else
84.                              push(&s1,post[i]-'0');
85.
86.                      i++;
87.              }
88.              ans = pop(&s1);
89.              return (ans);
90.      }
91.      int evalpre(char pre[])
92.      {
93.              struct stack s1;
94.              int i,a,b,ans;
95.              s1.top = -1;
96.              i = 0;
97.              while(pre[i] != '\0')
98.                      i++;
99.              i--;
100.             while(i>= 0)
101.             {
102.                     if(isoperator(pre[i]))
103.                     {
104.                             a = pop(&s1);
105.                             b = pop(&s1);
106.                             ans = eval(pre[i],a,b);
107.                             push(&s1,ans);
108.                     }
109.                     else
110.                     push(&s1,pre[i]-'0');
111.                     i--;
112.             }
113.             ans = pop(&s1);
114.             return (ans);
115.     }
```

4.   Print the reverse of a string:-

```
1.      #include<stdio.h>
2.      #include<conio.h>
3.      #define MAXSTK 10
4.      struct stack
5.      {
6.              int data[MAXSTK];
7.              int top;
8.      };
9.      void rev( char [] );
10.     void push(struct stack *,int );
11.     int pop(struct stack *);
12.     void main()
13.     {
14.             char str[10]="";
15.             clrscr();
16.             printf("Enter a String:- ");
17.             gets(str);
18.             printf("Reverse of Entered String:- ");
19.             rev(str);
20.             getch();
21.     }
22.     void rev(char str[])
23.     {
24.             struct stack s1;
25.             int i = 0;
26.             s1.top = -1;
27.             while(str[i]!='\0')
28.                 push(&s1,str[i++]);
29.             while(s1.top != -1)
30.                 printf("%c",pop(&s1));
31.     }
32.     void push(struct stack *p,int val)
33.     {
34.             if(p->top == MAXSTK-1)
35.                 {
36.                     printf("Stack is Full.");
37.                     return;
38.                 }
39.             p->top++;
40.             p->data[p->top]=val;
41.     }
42.     int pop(struct stack *p)
43.     {
44.             int val;
```

```
45.              if(p->top == -1)
46.                  {
47.                      printf("Stack is Empty.");
48.                      return NULL;
49.                  }
50.              val=p->data[p->top];
51.              p->top--;
52.              return(val);
53.      }
```

5.   Check whether a equation is Palindrome or not:-

```
1.      #include<stdio.h>
2.      #include<conio.h>
3.      #define MAXSTK 10
4.      struct stack
5.      {
6.              int data[MAXSTK];
7.              int top;
8.      };
9.      int check( char [] );
10.     void push(struct stack *,int );
11.     int pop(struct stack *);
12.     void main()
13.     {
14.             char str[10]="";
15.             int flag = 0;
16.             clrscr();
17.             printf("Enter a String:- ");
18.             gets(str);
19.             flag =  check(str);
20.             if(flag == 1)
21.                     printf("String is Palindrome.");
22.             else
23.                     printf("String is not Palindrome.");
24.             getch();
25.     }
26.     int check(char str[])
27.     {
28.             struct stack s1;
29.             int i = 0;
30.             s1.top = -1;
31.             while(str[i]!='\0')
32.                 push(&s1,str[i++]);
33.             i = 0;
34.             while(str[i]!='\0')
```

```
35.                  {
36.                          if(str[i]!=pop(&s1))
37.                                  return (0);
38.                          i++;
39.                  }
40.          return(1);
41.  }
42.  void push(struct stack *p,int val)
43.  {
44.          if(isfull(*p))
45.             {
46.                  printf("Stack is Full.");
47.                  return;
48.             }
49.          p->top++;
50.          p->data[p->top]=val;
51.  }
52.  int pop(struct stack *p)
53.  {
54.          int val;
55.          if(isempty(*p))
56.             {
57.                  printf("Stack is Empty.");
58.                  return NULL;
59.             }
60.          val=p->data[p->top];
61.          p->top--;
62.          return(val);
63.  }
64.  int isfull(struct stack p)
65.  {
66.          return(p.top==MAXSTK-1);
67.  }
68.  int isempty(struct stack p)
69.  {
70.          return(p.top==-1);
71.  }
```

6.   Tower of Hanoi Recursive:-

```
1.      #include<stdio.h>
2.      #include<conio.h>
3.      void tower(int, char, char, char);
4.      void main()
5.      {
6.              int n;
7.              clrscr();
8.              printf("Enter how many disks");
9.              scanf("%d",&n);
10.             tower(n,'A','B','C');
11.             getch();
12.     }
13.     void tower(int n, char beg, char aux, char end)
14.     {
15.             if(n == 1)
16.             {
17.     printf("Disk 1 is transferred from %c to %c\n",beg,end);
18.                     return;
19.             }
20.             tower(n-1,beg,end,aux);
21.             printf("Disk %d is transferred from %c to %c\n",n,beg,end);
22.             tower(n-1,aux,beg,end);
23.     }
```

7.   Tower of Hanoi Non-Recursive Using Stack:-
```
1.      #include<stdio.h>
2.      #include<conio.h>
3.      #define MAXSTK 10
4.      struct item
5.      {
6.              int n;
7.              char beg;
8.              char end;
9.              char aux;
10.             char add;
11.     };
12.     struct stack
13.     {
14.             int top;
15.             struct item data[MAXSTK];
16.     };
17.     void push(struct stack *, struct item);
18.     struct item pop(struct stack *);
19.     void tower(int, char, char, char);
```

```
20.     void main()
21.     {
22.             int n;
23.             clrscr();
24.             printf("Enter how many rings");
25.             scanf("%d",&n);
26.             tower(n,'A','B','C');
27.             getch();
28.     }
29.     void push(struct stack *p, struct item it)
30.     {
31.             if(p->top == MAXSTK-1)
32.             {
32.                     printf("Stack is full");
34.                     return;
35.             }
36.             p->top++;
37.             p->data[p->top] = it;
38.     }
39.     struct item pop(struct stack *p)
40.     {
50.     struct item it;
51.             if(p->top == -1)
52.             {
53.                     printf("Stack is empty");
54.                     return it;
55.             }
56.             it = p->data[p->top];
57.             p->top--;
58.             return (it);
59.     }
60.     void tower(int n, char beg, char aux, char end)
61.     {
62.         struct stack s1;
63.         struct item currentitem;
64.         int t;
65.         s1.top = -1;
66.       step1:
67.             if(n == 1)
68.             {
69.     printf("\n Disk No 1 is transferred from %c to %c",beg,end);
70.                     goto step5;
71.             }
72.       step2:
73.             currentitem.n = n;
74.             currentitem.beg = beg;
```

```
75.              currentitem.end = end;
76.              currentitem.aux = aux;
77.              currentitem.add = 3;
78.              push(&s1,currentitem);
79.              n--;
80.              t = end;
81.              end = aux;
82.              aux = t;
83               goto step1;
84.      step3:
85.     printf("\n Disk no %d is transferred from %c to %c",n,beg,end);
86.      step4:
87.              currentitem.n = n;
88.              currentitem.beg = beg;
89.              currentitem.end = end;
90.              currentitem.aux = aux;
91.              currentitem.add = 5;
92.              push(&s1,currentitem);
93.              n--;
94.              t = aux;
95.              aux = beg;
96.              beg = t;
97.              goto step1;
98.      step5:
99.              if( s1.top == -1)
100.                     return;
101.             currentitem = pop(&s1);
102.             n = currentitem.n;
103.             beg = currentitem.beg;
104.             end = currentitem.end;
105.             aux = currentitem.aux;
106.             switch(currentitem.add)
107.             {
108.             case 3:
109.                     goto step3;
110.             case 5:
111.                     goto step5;
112.             }
113.     }
```

8.   Parenthesis Matching:

```
1.      #include<stdio.h>
2.      #include<conio.h>
3.      #define MAXSTK 10
4.      struct stack
5.      {
6.              int data[MAXSTK];
7.              int top;
8.      };
9.      int valid_eq(char []);
10.     void push(struct stack *,int );
11.     int pop(struct stack *);
12.     void main()
13.     {
14.             int flag = 0;
15.             char eq[20] = "";
16.             clrscr();
17.             printf("Enter a Equation:- ");
18.             gets(eq);
19.             flag=valid_eq(eq);
20.             if(flag==1)
21.                     printf("Entered Equation is valid.");
22.             else
23.                     printf("Entered Equation is not valid.");
24.             getch();
25.     }
26.     int valid_eq(char eq[])
27.     {
28.             struct stack s1;
29.             int i = 0;
30.             char ch ;
31.             s1.top = -1;
32.             while(eq[i]!='\0')
33.             {
34.                     if(eq[i] == '(')
35.                       push(&s1,eq[i]);
36.                     else if(eq[i] == ')')
37.                     {
38.                     if(s1.top == -1)
39.                             return(0);
40.                     else
41.                             ch=pop(&s1);
42.                     }
43.                     i++;
44.             }
```

```
45.            if(s1.top != -1)
46.                    return(0);
47.            else
48.                    return(1);
49.    }
50.    void push(struct stack *p,int val)
51.    {
52.            if(p->top == MAXSTK-1)
53.              {
54.                    printf("Stack is Full.");
55.                    return;
56.              }
57.            p->top++;
58.            p->data[p->top]=val;
59.    }
60.    int pop(struct stack *p)
61.    {
62.            int val;
63.            if(p->top == -1)
64.              {
65.                    printf("Stack is Empty.");
66.                    return NULL;
67.              }
68.            val=p->data[p->top];
69.            p->top--;
70.            return(val);
71.    }
```

CHAPTER
∞ **6** ∞
(QUEUE)

Introduction-

All of us are familiar with queues. In simple terms a queue is a line of persons waiting for their turn at some service counter / window. A service counter can be ticketing window of a cinema hall, a ticketing window of a bus stand, railway station, a service counter of a bank, a service counter of gas agency, a fees deposit counter in a college, etc..

Depending on the type of service provided by the service counter and the number of persons interested in this service, there can be queues of varying length. The service at the service counter is provided on the Fist-In-First-Out (FIFO) basis i.e. in order of their arrival in the queue.

Definition:
A queue is a linear list in which insertions can take place at one end on the list called the rear of the list and deletions can take place only at the other end called the front of the list. The behavior of a queue is like a First-In-First-Out (FIFO) system

Operations on queues: The following operations are performed on queues.

1.   AddQ (QUEUE, ITEM) - To insert element in the end of a queue.
2.   DelQ (QUEUE) - To access and remove front element of queue.
        All of these operation runs in O(1) time.

Note:
        If the queue is empty then it is not possible to delete the element from queue. Likewise if the queue is full then it is not possible to add a new element into the queue.

Representation of Queue in memory:

Queue like stacks can also be represented in memory using a linear array or a linear linked list.

Applications of Queues:-

        Some of the applications of queues are listed below:

*   There are several algorithms that use queues to solve problems efficiently.

*   When the jobs are submitted to a networked printer they are arranged in order of arrival. Thus, essentially jobs sent to a printer are placed on a queue.

*   There is a kind of computer network where disk is attached to one computer known as file server. Users on other computers are given access to files on a first-come first-served basis, so the data structure is a queue.

*   Virtually every real-life line (supposed to be) a queue. For example, lines at ticket counters at cinema halls, railway stations, bus stands, etc., are queues, because the service (i.e. ticket) is provided on fist-come first-served basis.

Type of Queues:

1.   Linear Queue.
2.   Circular Queue.
3.   Double Ended Queue.
4.   Multi-Queue.
5.   Priority Queue

LINEAR QUEUE:

To implement a queue we need variables called front and rear that holds the index of the first and last element of the queue and an array to hold the elements of the queue. When we add an element rear increases and when we remove an element front increases but this method however is too inefficient because if the last element is occupied a new value cannot be inserted even if some elements are empty in the Queue.

However this limitation can be overcome by moving the elements forward such that the second element of the queue goes to position with index 1 and the rest of the elements move accordingly.

And finally the front and rear variables are adjusted appropriately. But this operation may be very time consuming if the length of the linear queue is very long.

As mentioned earlier this limitation can be overcome if we treat the queue position with index 1 comes immediately after the last queue position with index 1 comes immediately after the last queue position with index MAXQ. The resulting queue is known as circular queue.

CIRCULAR QUEUE:

In Circular Queue the array that holds the queue is viewed as a circle rather than as a straight line. That is we imagine the first element of the array (that is the element at position 1) as immediately following its last element. This implies that even if the last element is occupied a new value can be inserted behind it in the first element of the array as long as that first element is empty.

DOUBLE ENDED QUEUE:

A DE Queue is a kind of queue in which elements can be added or removed from at either end but not in the middle. The term deque is a contraction of the name double-ended queue.

There are two variations of a DE-Queue these are:

- **Input-restricted DEQUEUE:-**Which allows insertions only at one end but allows deletions at both ends.

- **Output-restricted DEQUEUE:-**Which allows insertions at both ends but allows deletions only at one end.

MULTI QUEUE:-

Maintaining more than one Queue in a single array to save memory space is called as multiqueue. First Queue starts from Left to Right in the array and second Queue starts from Right to Left. In this first Queue can use extra space of second Queue (if available) and vice versa.

PRIORITY QUEUE:

A priorities queue is a kind of queue in which each element is assigned a priority and the order in which elements are deleted and processed comes from the following rules:

1. An element with highest priority is processed first before any element of lower priority.

2. Two or more elements with the same priority are processed according to the order in which they were added to the queue.

There can be different criteria's for determining the priority. Some of them are summarized below:

1. A shortest job is given higher priority over the longer one.

2. An important job is given the higher priority over a routine type job. For example, a transaction for on-line booking of an order is given preference over payroll processing.

3. In a commercial computer center the amount we pay for the job can determine priority for our job. Pay more to get higher priority for our job.

Representing a priority queue in memory:

There are various ways representing (maintaining) a priority queue in memory.
These are:

1. Using a linear linked list.

2. Using multiple queues one for each priority

3. Using a heap.

Linear Linked list Representation:

In this representation each node of the linked list will have three field:

1. An information field info that hold the element of the queue,

2. A priority field prn that holds the priority number of the element,and

3. A next pointer filed link that holds the pointer to the next element of the queue.

Further a node X precedes a node Y in the linear list if either node X has higher priority than Y or both nodes have same priority but X was added to the list before Y.

In a given system we can assign higher priority to lower number or higher number. Therefore, if higher priority is for lower number we have to maintain linear linked lists sorted on ascending order of the priority **(Ascending priority queue APQ)**.

However if higher priority is for higher number we have to maintain linear linked lists sorted on descending order of the priority **(Descending priority queue DPQ)..** This way the element to be processed next is available as the first element of the linked list.

Heap representation of a priority queue:-

A heap is a complete binary tree and with the additional property the root element is either smallest or largest from its children If root element of the heap is smallest from its children it is known as min heap.

If root element of the heap is largest from its children it is known as max heap. A priority queue having highest priority for lower number can be represented using min heap and a priority queue having highest priority for highest number can be represented using max heap.

Algorithms:

1.LINEAR QUEUE:

ADDQ (QUEUE, MAXQ, FRONT, REAR, ITEM)

This procedure inserts a new ITEM at the rear end of the queue.

1.   [Check Overflow condition.]
        If REAR = MAXQ, then: Write: OVERFLOW and Return.
2.   [Increment REAR]
        If FRONT:= 0, then: [Queue initially empty.]
                Set FRONT:= 1 and REAR:= 1.
        Else:
                Set REAR:= REAR + 1.
        [End of If structure]
3.   Set QUEUE [REAR]:= ITEM. [This inserts new element.]
4.   Return.

DELQ (QUEUE , FRONT , REAR , ITEM)

This procedure deletes an element from a queue and assigns it to the variable ITEM.

1.   [Queue already empty ?]
        If FRONT:= 0 , then: Write: UNDERFLOW, and Return.
2.   [Remove an element.]
        Set ITEM:= QUEUE [FRONT].
3.   If FRONT = REAR then: [If Removing the last element.]
                Set FRONT:= 0, REAR:= 0.
        Else:
                Set FRONT:= FRONT + 1.
        [End of If Structure]
4.   Return.

2.CIRCULAR QUEUE:

ADDCIRQ (QUEUE , MAXQ , FRONT , REAR , ITEM)

This procedure inserts an element ITEM into a circular queue.

1.   [Check for the Overflow.]
        If FRONT = 1 and REAR = MAXQ, or FRONT = REAR + 1, then:
                Write: OVERFLOW, and Return.
        [End of If structure]

2.   [Find new value of REAR.]
        If FRONT:= 0, then: [Queue initially empty.]
                Set FRONT:= 1 and REAR:= 1.
        Else if REAR:= MAXQ, then:
                Set REAR:= 1.
        Else:
                Set REAR:= REAR + 1.
        [End of if structure.]
3.   Set QUEUE [REAR]:= ITEM. [This inserts new element.]
4.   Return.

DELCIRQ (QUEUE , MAXQ , FRONT , REAR , ITEM)

This procedure deletes an element from a circular queue and assigns
it to the variable ITEM.

1.   [Queue already empty ?]
        If FRONT:= 0 , then: Write: UNDERFLOW, and Return.
2.   Set ITEM:= QUEUE [FRONT].
3.   [Find new value of FRONT.]
        If FRONT = REAR, then: [Queue has only one element to remove.]
                Set FRONT:= 0 and REAR:= 0.
        Else If FRONT = MAXQ, then:
                Set FRONT:= 1.
        Else:
                Set FRONT:= FRONT + 1.
        [End of if structure.]
4.   Return.

3.DE-QUEUE:

LEFTADD_DEQ (QUEUE , MAXQ , LEFT , RIGHT , ITEM)

This procedure inserts an element ITEM from left into a DE Queue.

1.   [Check for the Overflow.]
        If (LEFT = 1 and RIGHT = MAXQ) or LEFT = RIGHT + 1, then:
                Write: OVERFLOW , and Return.
        [End of If structure]
2.   [Find new value of LEFT.]
        If LEFT = 0, then:
                Set LEFT:= MAXQ, RIGHT:= MAXQ.
        Else If LEFT = 1, then:
                Set LEFT := MAXQ.
        Else:
                Set LEFT:= LEFT - 1.

[End of if structure.]
3.   Set QUEUE [LEFT]:= ITEM. [This inserts new element.]
4.   Return.

RIGHTADD_DEQ (QUEUE , MAXQ , LEFT , RIGHT , ITEM)

This procedure inserts an element ITEM from right into a dequeue.

1.   [Check for the Overflow.]
        If (LEFT = 1 and RIGHT = MAXQ) or LEFT = RIGHT + 1, then:
                Write: OVERFLOW , and Return.
2.   [Find new value of RIGHT.]
        If RIGHT = 0, then:
                Set LEFT: =1, RIGHT: = 1.
        Else If RIGHT = MAXQ, then
                Set Right:= 1.
        Else:
                Set Right: = Right + 1.
        [End of If Structure]
3.   Set QUEUE [RIGHT]:= ITEM. [This inserts new element]
4.   Return.

RIGHTDEL_DEQ (QUEUE , MAXQ , LEFT , RIGHT , ITEM)

This procedure deletes an element from a dequeue from right and assigns it to the variable ITEM.
1.   [Queue already empty ?]
        If LEFT = 0 , then: Write: UNDERFLOW, and Return.
2.   Set ITEM:= QUEUE [RIGHT].
3.   [Find new value of RIGHT.]
         If RIGHT = LEFT, then:
                Set RIGHT:= 0 and LEFT:= 0.
        Else If RIGHT = 1, then:
                Set RIGHT:= MAXQ.
        Else:
                Set RIGHT:= RIGHT - 1.
        [End of if structure.]
        Return.

LEFTDEL_DEQ (QUEUE , MAXQ , LEFT , RIGHT , ITEM)

This procedure deletes an element from a dequeue from left and assigns it to the variable ITEM.

1.   [Queue already empty ?]
        If LEFT = 0 , then: Write: UNDERFLOW, and Return.
2.   Set ITEM:= QUEUE [LEFT].
3.   [Find new value of LEFT.]
        If LEFT = RIGHT, then:
                Set RIGHT:= 0 and LEFT:= 0.
        Else If LEFT = MAXQ, then:
                Set LEFT:= 1.
        Else:
                Set LEFT:= LEFT + 1.
        [End of if structure.]
    4. Return.

4.MULTI QUEUE:

ADDFIRSTQ (QUEUE, FRONT1, REAR1, REAR2, ITEM)

        This procedure inserts an element ITEM in a first queue. Initially
        FRONT1 and REAR1 are initialized to zero when first queue is empty.

1.   [Check for the Overflow.]
        If (REAR1 + 1) = REAR2, then: Write: OVERFLOW , and Return.
2.   If FRONT =0, then:
                Set FRONT1: =1 and REAR: =1.
        Else:
                Set REAR1: = REAR1+1.
        [End of If Structure]
3..   [Find new value of REAR1.]
        Set REAR1:= REAR1 + 1.
4.   Set QUEUE [REAR1]:= ITEM. [This inserts new element.]
5.   Return.

DELFIRSTQ(QUEUE, MAXQ, FRONT1, REAR1, ITEM)
        This procedure deletes an element from a first queue and assigns it to
        the variable ITEM.

1.   [Queue already empty ?]
        If FRONT1 = 0 , then: Write: UNDERFLOW, and Return.
2.   Set ITEM:= QUEUE [FRONT1].
3.   [Find new value of FRONT1.]
        If FRONT1 = REAR1, then:
                Set FRONT1:= 0 and REAR1:= 0.
        Else:
                Set FRONT1:= FRONT1 + 1.
        [End of if structure.]
4.   Return.

ADDSECONDQ(QUEUE,MAXQ,FRONT1,REAR1,FRONT2,REAR2,ITEM)

This procedure inserts an element ITEM in a second queue. Initially FRONT1 and REAR1 are initialized to MAXQ + 1 when first queue is empty.

1.   [Check for the Overflow.]
     If (REAR1 + 1) = REAR2, then: Write: OVERFLOW , and Return.
2.   If REAR2 = MAXQ + 1, then:
          Set FRONT2: = MAXQ, REAR2: = MAXQ.
     Else:
          Set REAR: = REAR- 1.
     [End of If Structure]
3.   Set QUEUE [REAR2]:= ITEM. [This inserts new element.]
4.   Return.

DELSECONDQ (QUEUE, MAXQ, FRONT1, REAR1, FRONT2, REAR2, ITEM)

This procedure deletes an element from second queue and assigns it to the variable ITEM.

1.   [Queue already empty ?]
     If FRONT2 = MAXQ+1 , then: Write: UNDERFLOW, and Return.
2.   Set ITEM:= QUEUE [FRONT2].
3.   [Find new value of FRONT2.]
     If FRONT2 = REAR2, then:
          Set FRONT2:= MAXQ+1 and REAR2:= MAXQ+1.
     Else:
          Set FRONT2:= FRONT2 - 1.
     [End of if structure.]
4.   Return.

5.PRIORITY QUEUE:

ADDPQ (PQUEUE , MAXQ, FRONT, REAR, PRIORITY, ITEM, MAXP)

This procedure inserts an element in a priority queue .

1. If PRIORITY > MAXP , then: Write: "Such a priority queue does not exist", and Return.
     [Queue already full ?]

2. If (FRONT[PRIORITY] = 1 and REAR[PRIORITY] = MAXQ) or FRONT[PRIORITY] =

(REAR[PRIORITY] + 1) then Write: "This priority queue is full" and Return.

3. [Find new value of REAR.]
   If FRONT[PRIORITY] := 0, then:

       Set FRONT[PRIORITY] := 1, REAR[PRIORITY] := 1

   Else If REAR[PRIORITY] = MAXQ, then:

       Set REAR[PRIORITY] := 1.

   Else:
       Set REAR[PRIORITY] = REAR[PRIORITY] + 1.

   [End of if structure.]

4. Set PQUEUE[PRIORITY][REAR[PRIORITY]] := ITEM.

5. Return.

DELPQ (PQUEUE , MAXQ, FRONT, REAR, ITEM, N)

This procedure deletes an element in a priority queue .

1.   [Finding the smallest queue which is not empty ?]
   Set PRIORITY = 1.
   Repeat steps while REAR[PRIORITY] = 0 AND PRIORITY<= N
       Set PRIORITY = PRIORITY + 1.
   [End of loop]

2.   If PRIORITY > N then Write: "Priority queue is empty" and Return

3.   Set ITEM:= PQUEUE[PRIORITY][FRONT[PRIORITY]].

4.   [Find new value of FRONT and REAR.]
   If FRONT[PRIORITY] = REAR[PRIORITY], then:

       Set FRONT[PRIORITY] := 0 , REAR[PRIORITY] := 0.

   Else If FRONT[PRIORITY] = MAXQ:
       Set FRONT[PRIORITY] = 1.

   Else:
       Set FRONT[PRIORITY] = Set FRONT[PRIORITY] + 1.
   [End of If structure].

5.   Return.

1.Linear Queue:

```
1.      #include<stdio.h>
2.      #include<conio.h>
3.      #define MAXQ 10
4.      struct queue
5.      {
6.              int data[MAXQ];
7.              int front,rear;
8.      };
9.      void addq(struct queue *,int );
10.     int delq(struct queue *);
11.     void main()
12.     {
13.             int ch,item;
14.             struct queue q1;
15.             q1.front = q1.rear = -1;
16.             do
17.             {
18.                     clrscr();
19.                     printf("\t\t\tMAIN MENU\n");
20.                     printf("\t\t\t********\n\n");
21.                     printf("\t\t 1.Add in a queue.\n");
22.                     printf("\t\t 2 Delete from a queue.\n");
23.                     printf("\t\t 3.Exit.\n\n");
24.                     printf("\t\t Enter your choice:- ");
25.                     scanf("%d",&ch);
26.                     clrscr();
27.                     switch(ch)
28.                     {
29.                             case 1:
30.                     printf("Enter the value which is to be Add:- ");
31.                                     scanf("%d",&item);
32.                                     addq(&q1,item);
33.                                     break;
34.                             case 2:
35.                                     item=delq(&q1);
36.                                     if(item != NULL)
37.                     printf("Deleted Value==> %d",item);
38.                                     break;
39.                             case 3:
40.                                     break;
41.                             default:
```

```
42.                    printf("Wrong Choice !.Try Again .");
43.                    }
44.                    getch();
45.             }while(ch!=3);
46.     }
47.     void addq(struct queue *p,int item)
48.     {
49.             if(p->rear == MAXQ-1)
50.             {
51.                    printf("Queue is Full.");
52.                    return;
53.             }
54.             if(p->front==-1)
55.                    p->front = p->rear = 0;
56.             else
57.                    p->rear++;
58.             p->data[p->rear]=item;
59.     }
60.     int delq(struct queue *p)
61.     {
62.             int item;
63.             if(p->front == -1)
64.             {
65.             printf("Queue is Empty.");
66.             return(NULL);
67.             }
68.             item=p->data[p->front];
69.             if(p->front==p->rear)
70.                    p->front=p->rear=-1;
71.             else
72.                    p->front++;
73.             return(item);
74.     }
```

2. Circular Queue:

```
1.      #include<stdio.h>
2.      #include<conio.h>
3.      #define MAXQ 10
4.      struct cirqueue
5.      {
6.              int data[MAXQ];
7.              int front,rear;
8.      };
9.      void addq(struct cirqueue *,int );
10.     int delq(struct cirqueue *);
```

```
11.              void main()
12.        {
13.              int ch,item;
14.              struct cirqueue q1;
15.              q1.front = q1.rear = -1;
16.              do
17.              {
18.                      clrscr();
19.                      printf("\t\t\tMAIN MENU\n");
20.                      printf("\t\t\t********\n\n");
21.                      printf("\t\t 1.Add in a queue.\n");
22.                      printf("\t\t 2.Delete from a queue.\n");
23.                      printf("\t\t 3.Exit.\n\n");
24.                      printf("\t\t Enter your choice:- ");
25.                      scanf("%d",&ch);
26.                      clrscr();
27.                      switch(ch)
28.                      {
29.                              case 1:
30.                      printf("Enter the value which is to be Add:- ");
31.                                      scanf("%d",&item);
32.                                      addq(&q1,item);
33.                                      break;
34.                              case 2:
35.                                      item = delq(&q1);
36.                                      if(item!=NULL)
37.                      printf("Deleted Value ==> %d",item);
38.                                      break;
39.                              case 3:
40.                                      break;
41.                              default:
42.                      printf("Wrong Choice !.Try Again .");
43.                      }
44.                      getch();
45.              }while(ch!=3);
46.        }
47     .void addq(struct cirqueue *p,int item)
48.        {
49.        if(p->rear==MAXQ-1 && p->front==0 || p->rear+1==p->front)
50.              {
51.                      printf("Queue is full\n");
52.                      return;
53.              }
54.              if(p->front == -1)
55.                      p->front = p->rear = 0;
56.              else if(p->rear == MAXQ-1)
```

```
57.                          p->rear = 0;
58.            else
59.                          p->rear++;
60.                  p->data[p->rear] = item;
61.       }
62.       int delq(struct cirqueue *p)
63.       {
64.              int item;
65.              if(p->front == -1)
66.              {
67.                      printf("Queue is Empty.");
68.                      return(NULL);
69.              }
70.              item = p->data[p->front];
71.              if(p->front == p->rear)
72.                      p->front = p->rear = -1;
73.              else if(p->front == MAXQ-1)
74.                      p->front = 0;
75.              else
76.                      p->front++;
77.              return(item);
78.       }
```

3.   Multi Queue (2 Queues in a single array):

```
1.       #include<stdio.h>
2.       #include<conio.h>
3.       #define MAXQ 20
4.       struct mulqueue
5.       {
6.              int data[MAXQ];
7.              int front1,rear1;
8.              int front2,rear2;
9.       };
10.      void addfq(struct mulqueue *,int );
11.      void addsq(struct mulqueue *,int );
12.      int delfq(struct mulqueue *);
13.      int delsq(struct mulqueue *);
14.      void main()
15.      {
16.              int ch,item;
17.              struct mulqueue q;
18.              q.front1 = q.rear1 = -1;
19.              q.front2 = q.rear2 = MAXQ;
20.              do
21.              {
```

```c
22.                     clrscr();
23.                     printf("\t\t\tMAIN MENU\n");
24.                     printf("\t\t\t*********\n\n");
25.                     printf("\t\t 1.Add in a First queue.\n");
26.                     printf("\t\t 2.Add in a Second queue.\n");
27.                     printf("\t\t 3.Delete from a First queue.\n");
28.                     printf("\t\t 4.Delete from a Second queue.\n");
29.                     printf("\t\t 5.Exit.\n\n");
30.                     printf("\t\t Enter your choice:- ");
31.                     scanf("%d",&ch);
32.                     clrscr();
33.                     switch(ch)
34.                     {
35.                             case 1:
36.                                     printf("Enter the value :- ");
37.                                     scanf("%d",&item);
38.                                     addfq(&q,item);
39.                                     break;
40.                             case 2:
41.                                     printf("Enter the value :- ");
42.                                     scanf("%d",&item);
43.                                     addsq(&q,item);
44.                                     break;
45.                             case 3:
46.                                     item = delfq(&q);
47.                                     if(item != NULL)
48.                             printf("Deleted Value ==> %d",item);
49.                                     break;
50.                             case 4:
51.                                     item = delsq(&q);
52.                                     if(item != NULL)
53.                             printf("Deleted Value ==> %d",item );
54.                                     break;
55.                             case 5:
56.                                     break;
57.                             default:
58.                             printf("Wrong Choice !.Try Again .");
59.                     }
60.                     getch();
61.             }while(ch!=5);
62.     }
63.     void addfq(struct mulqueue *p,int item)
64.     {
65.             if(p->rear1 + 1 == p->rear2)
66.             {
67.                     printf("Multi Queue is Full.");
```

```
68.                     getch();
69.                     return;
70.             }
71.             if(p->front1 == -1)
72.                     p->front1 = p->rear1 = 0;
73.             else
74.                     p->rear1++;
75.             p->data[p->rear1] = item;
76.     }
77.     void addsq(struct mulqueue *p,int item)
78.     {
79.             if(p->rear1 + 1 == p->rear2)
80.             {
81.                     printf("Multi Queue is Full.");
82.                     getch();
83.                     return;
84.             }
85.             if(p->front2 == MAXQ)
86.                     p->front2 = p->rear2 = MAXQ-1;
87.             else
88.                     p->rear2--;
89.             p->data[p->rear2] = item;
90.     }
91.     int delfq(struct mulqueue *p)
92.     {
93.             int item;
94.             if(p->front1 == -1)
95.             {
96.                     printf("First Queue is Empty.");
97.                     return(NULL);
98.             }
99.             item = p->data[p->front1];
100.            if(p->front1 == p->rear1)
101.                    p->front1 = p->rear1 = -1;
102.            else
103.                    p->front1++;
104.            return(item);
105.    }
106.    int delsq(struct mulqueue *p)
107.    {
108.            int item;
109.            if(p->front2 == MAXQ)
110.            {
111.                    printf("Second Queue is Empty.");
112.                    return(NULL);
113.            }
```

```
114.            item = p->data[p->front2];
115.            if(p->front2 == p->rear2)
116.                    p->front2 = p->rear2 = MAXQ;
117.            else
118.                    p->front2--;
119.            return(item);
120.    }
```

4.   DeQueue - Double Ended Queue:

```
1.      #include<stdio.h>
2.      #include<conio.h>
3.      #define MAXQ 10
4.      struct queue
5.      {
6.              int data[MAXQ];
7.              int left,right;
8.      };
9.      void addr(struct queue *,int );
10.     void addl(struct queue *,int );
11.     int delr(struct queue *);
12.     int dell(struct queue *);
13.     void main()
14.     {
15.             int ch,item;
16.             struct queue q;
17.             q.left = q.right = -1;
18.             do
19.             {
20.                     clrscr();
21.                     printf("\t\t\tMAIN MENU\n");
22.                     printf("\t\t\t*********\n\n");
23.                     printf("\t\t 1.Add in Right in a queue.\n");
24.                     printf("\t\t 2.Add in Left in a queue.\n");
25.                     printf("\t\t 3.Delete from Right from a queue.\n");
26.                     printf("\t\t 4.Delete from Left from a queue.\n");
27.                     printf("\t\t 5.Exit.\n\n");
28.                     printf("\t\t Enter your choice:- ");
29.                     scanf("%d",&ch);
30.                     clrscr();
31.                     switch(ch)
32.                     {
33.                             case 1:
34.                                     printf("Enter the item:- ");
35.                                     scanf("%d",&item);
36.                                     addr(&q,item);
```

```
37.                                             break;
38.                             case 2:
39.                                     printf("Enter the item:- ");
40.                                     scanf("%d",&item);
41.                                     addl(&q,item);
42.                                     break;
43.                             case 3:
44.                                     item = delr(&q);
45.                                     if(item != NULL)
46.                             printf("Deleted Value ==> %d",item);
47.                                     break;
48.                             case 4:
49.                                     item = dell(&q);
50.                                     if(item != NULL)
51.                             printf("Deleted Value ==> %d",item);
52.                                     break;
53.                             case 5:
54.                                     break;
55.                             default:
56.                             printf("Wrong Choice !.Try Again .");
57.                     }
58.                             getch();
59.             }while(ch!=5);
60.     }
61.     void addr(struct queue *p,int item)
62.     {
63.             if(p->left == (p->right + 1) % MAXQ)
64.             {
65.                     printf("Dequeue is Full.");
66.                     return;
67.             }
68.             if(p->right == -1)
69.                     p->left = p->right = 0;
70.             else if(p->right == MAXQ-1)
71                     p->right = 0;
72.             else
73.                     p->right++;
74.             p->data[p->right] = item;
75.     }
76.     void addl(struct queue *p,int item)
77.     {
78.             if(p->left == (p->right + 1) % MAXQ)
79.             {
80.                     printf("Dequeue is Full.");
81.                     return;
82.             }
```

```
83.              if(p->left == -1)
84.                      p->left = p->right = MAXQ - 1;
85.              else if(p->left == 0)
86.                      p->left = MAXQ - 1;
87.              else
88.                      p->left--;
89.              p->data[p->left] = item;
90.      }
91.      int delr(struct queue *p)
92.      {
93.              int item = 0;
94.              if(p->left ==  -1)
95.              {
96.                      printf("Dequeue is Empty.");
97.                      return NULL;
98.              }
99.              item = p->data[p->right];
100.             if(p->right == p->left)
101.                     p->right = p->left = -1;
102.             else if(p->right == 0)
103.                     p->right = MAXQ - 1;
104.             else
105.                     p->right--;
106.             return(item);
107.     }
108.     int dell(struct queue *p)
109.     {
110.             int item = 0;
111.             if(p->left ==  -1)
112.             {
113.                     printf("Dequeue is Empty.");
114.                     return NULL;
115.             }
116.             item = p->data[p->left];
117.             if(p->left == p->right)
118.                     p->right = p->left = -1;
119.             else if(p->left == MAXQ - 1)
120.                     p->left = 0;
121.             else
122.                     p->left++;
123.             return(item);
124.     }
```

5.   Ascending Priority Queue using multiple circular queues:

```
1.      #include<stdio.h>
2.      #include<conio.h>
3.      #define MAXQ 10
4.      struct pqueue
5.      {
6.              int data[MAXQ];
7.              int front,rear;
8.      };
9.      void addpq(struct pqueue [],int ,int,int );
10.     int delpq(struct pqueue[],int);
11.     void main()
12.     {
13.             struct pqueue pq[10];
14.             int n,ch,item,p,i;
15.             clrscr();
16.             printf("Enter how many priorities");
17.             scanf("%d",&n);
18.             for(i=0;i<n;i++)
19.                     pq[i].front = pq[i].rear = -1;
20.             do
21.             {
22.                     clrscr();
23.                     printf("\n1. Insert \n2. Delete \n3. Exit");
24.                     printf("Enter your choice");
25.                     scanf("%d",&ch);
26.                     switch(ch)
27.                     {
28.                       case 1:
29.      .       printf("Enter item and its priority (from 1 to %d) ",n);
30.                             scanf("%d%d",&item,&p);
31.                             addpq(pq,item,p,n);
32.                             break;
33.                     case 2:
34.                             item=delpq(pq,n);
35.                             if(item != NULL)
36.                                     printf("%d",item);
37.                             break;
38.                     case 3:
39.                             break;
40.                     default:
41.                             printf("\nInvalid choice");
42.                     }
43.             getch();
44.             }while(ch!=3);
```

```
45.     }
46.     void addpq(struct pqueue pq[],int item,int p,int n)
47.     {
48.             if(p>n)
49.             {
50.                     printf("Such a priority queue does not exist");
51.                     return;
52.             }
53.             if(isfull(pq,p))
54.             {
55.                     printf("Queue with priority %d is full ",p);
56.                     return;
57.             }
58.             if(pq[p-1].rear == MAXQ-1)
59.                     pq[p-1].rear = 0;
60.             else
61.                     pq[p-1].rear++;
62.             pq[p-1].data[pq[p-1].rear] = item;
63.             if(pq[p-1].front == -1)
64.                     pq[p-1].front = 0;
65.     }
66.     int delpq(struct pqueue pq[],int n)
67.     {
68.             int item,p;
69.             for(p=1;p<=n;p++)
70.             {
71.                     if(!isempty(pq,p))
72.                             break;
73.             }
74.             if(p>n)
75.             {
76.                     printf("Queue is empty ");
77.                     return 0;
78.             }
79.             item = pq[p-1].data[pq[p-1].front];
80.             if(pq[p-1].front == pq[p-1].rear)
81.                     pq[p-1].front = pq[p-1].rear = -1;
82.             else if(pq[p-1].front == MAXQ-1)
83.                     pq[p-1].front = 0;
84.             else
85.                     pq[p-1].front++;
86.             return (item);
87.     }
88.     int isfull(struct pqueue pq[],int p)
89.     {
```

```
90.  if( (pq[p-1].front == 0 && pq[p-1].rear == MAXQ-1) || pq[p-1].rear+1 == 91.91
          pq[p-1].front)
91.               return (1);
92.       else
93.               return (0);
94.       }
95.       int isempty(struct pqueue pq[],int p)
96.       {
97.               if(pq[p-1].front == -1)
98.                       return(1);
99.               else
100.                      return(0);
101.      }
```

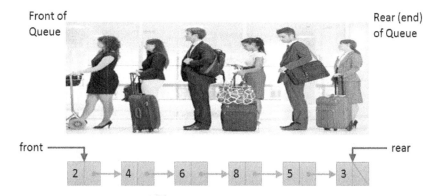

Front of Queue — Rear (end) of Queue

front — rear

2 → 4 → 6 → 8 → 5 → 3

Front pointer
*Pointing to **first** element of Queue*

Rear pointer
*Pointing to **Last** element of Queue*

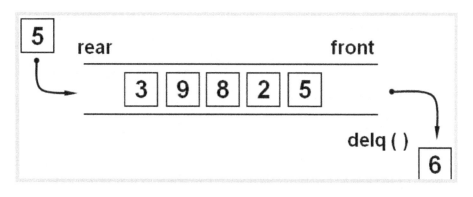

5   rear   front

3 9 8 2 5

delq ( )

6

CHAPTER
∞ 7 ∞
(LINK-LIST)

Introduction-

Data is organized into lists. One way to store such data is by means of arrays. The linear relationship between the data elements of an array is reflected by the physical relationship of the data in memory, not by any information contained in the data elements themselves.

This makes it easy to compute the address of an element in an array. On the other hand, arrays have certain disadvantages- e.g., it is relatively expensive to insert and delete elements in an array. Also since an array usually occupies a block of memory space, one cannot simply double or triple the size of an array when additional space is required. (For this reason, arrays are called dense lists and are said to be static data structures.)

Another way of storing a list in memory is to have each element in the list contain a field, called a link or pointer, which contains the address of the next element in the list. Thus successive elements in the list need not occupy adjacent space in memory. This will make it easier to insert and delete elements in the list. This latter type of data structure is called a **linked list.**

ADT LINKLIST:

A list of elements of type T is a finite sequence of elements of T together with the operations.

- Initialize the list to be empty.
- Determine whether the list is empty or not.
- Determine whether the list is full or not.
- Find the length of the list.
- Retrieve any node from the lust, provided that the list is not empty.
- Store a new node replacing the node at any position in the list, provided that the list is not empty.
- Insert a new node into the list at any position, provided that the list is not full.
- Deletes any node from the list, provided that the list is not empty.

Type of Linked List-

1. Singly Linked List or One-Way List.
2. Doubly Linked List or Two-Way List.
3. Circular Linked List.
4. Header Linked List.
5. Circular Header Linked List.

1.Singly Linked List-

A singly linked list, or one-way list, is a linear collection of data elements, called nodes, where the linear order is given by means of pointers. That is, each node is divided into two parts:

The first part contains the information of the element, and the second part, called the link field or next pointer field, contains the address of the next node in the list.

Another pointer variable called as START, is used that contains the address of the first element of the list. The last element of the linked list have NULL value in the link pointer field to mark the end of the list.

TRAVERSE (START, INFO, LINK)

Let LIST be a linked list in the memory. This algorithm traverses LIST, applying an operation PROCESS to each element of the LIST.

The variable PTR points to the node currently being processed.

1.   Set PTR: = START. [Initializes pointer PTR.]
2.   Repeat Steps 3 and 4 While PTR ≠ NULL:
3.   Apply PROCESS to INFO [PTR].
4.   Set PTR: = LINK [PTR].   [PTR now points to the next node.]
     [End of step 2 loop.]
5.   EXIT.

COUNT (START, INFO, LINK, CNT)

Let LIST be a linked list in the memory. This algorithm counts the number of nodes in the LIST and stores the result in CNT.

1.   Set CNT: = 0. [Initialize counter.]
2.   Set PTR: = START.   [Initializes pointer PTR.]

3.   Repeat Steps 4 and 5 While PTR ≠ NULL:

4   Set CNT: = CNT + 1.   [Increment counter by 1.]

5.   Set PTR: =LINK [PTR].   [PTR now points to the next node.]

     [End of step 2 loop.]
6.   EXIT.

SEARCH (START, INFO, LINK, ITEM, LOC)

Let LIST is a linked list in memory. This algorithm finds the location LOC of the node where ITEM first appears in LIST, or sets LOC: = NULL.

1.   Set PTR: =START.
2.   Repeat Step 3 While PTR ≠ NULL:
3.   If ITEM = INFO [PTR], then:
          Set LOC: =PTR, and Exit.
     Else:
          Set PTR: = LINK [PTR].
          [End of If structure.]
     [End of Step 2 loop.]
4.   [Search is unsuccessful.]
     Set LOC: = NULL.
5.   Exit.

SRCHSL (START, INFO, LINK, ITEM, LOC)

Let LIST is a sorted list in the memory. This algorithm finds the location LOC of the node where ITEM first appears in LIST, or set LOC: = NULL.

1.   Set PTR: = START.
2.   Repeat Step 3 While PTR ≠ NULL:
3.   If ITEM > INFO [PTR], then:
                 Set PTR: = LINK [PTR].   [PTR now points to the next node.]
                 Else If ITEM = INFO [PTR], then:
                         Set LOC: = PTR, and Exit. [Search is successful]
                 Else:
                 Set LOC: =NULL, and Exit. [ITEM now exceeds INFO [PTR].]
                 [End of If structure.]
                 [End of Step 2 loop.]
4.   Set LOC: =NULL.
5.   Exit.

ADDFIRST (START, INFO, LINK, AVAIL, ITEM)

This procedure adds a new node at the beginning of list.

START: - It has the address of first node
AVAIL: - It has the address of first free node in memory.

1.   [OVERFLOW?]
         If AVAIL = NULL, then: Write: OVERFLOW and Exit.
2.   [Remove the first node from AVAIL list.]
         Set NEW: = AVAIL, AVAIL: = LINK [AVAIL].
3.   Set INFO [NEW]: = ITEM.   [Copies new data into new node.]
4.   Set LINK [NEW]: = START. [New node now points to original first node.]
5.   Set START: = NEW. [Changes START so it points to the new node.]
6.   Exit.

APPEND (START, INFO, LINK, AVAIL, ITEM)

This procedure adds a new element at the end of LIST.
1.   [OVERFLOW?]
         If AVAIL = NULL, then: Write: OVERFLOW and Exit.
2.   [Remove the first node from AVAIL list.]
         Set NEW: = AVAIL, AVAIL : = LINK [AVAIL].
3.   Set INFO [NEW]: = ITEM.   [Copies new data into new node.]
4.   Set LINK [NEW]: = NULL.
5.   If START = NULL, then:
                 Set START: = NEW.
         Else:
                 Set PTR: = START.   [Initialize pointer.]
                 Repeat Step While LINK [PTR] ≠ NULL:
                         Set PTR: = LINK [PTR]. [End of loop]
                 Set LINK [PTR] : = NEW. [End of If structure.]
6.   Exit.

ADDAFTER (START, LINK, INFO, AVAIL, ITEM, POS)

This procedure adds a new element after the given position pos.

1.   Set PTR: = START.
2.   Repeat Steps For I: = 1 to POS – 1:
            Set PTR: = LINK [PTR].
      If PTR = NULL, then: Write: "Such a node does not exist " and Exit.
      [End of Step 2 loop.]
3.   [OVERFLOW?]
      If AVAIL = NULL, then: Write: OVERFLOW and Exit.
4.   [Remove the first node from AVAIL list.]
      Set NEW: = AVAIL, AVAIL: = LINK [AVAIL].
5.   Set INFO [NEW]: = ITEM.   [Copies new data into new node.]
6.   Set LINK [NEW]: = LINK [PTR].
7.   Set LINK [PTR]: = NEW.
8.   Exit.

INSLOC (START, INFO, LINK, AVAIL, ITEM)

This algorithm inserts ITEM into a sorted linked list.

1.   Call FIND (START, INFO, LINK, ITEM, LOC).
2.   [OVERFLOW?]
      If AVAIL = NULL, then: Write: OVERFLOW, and Exit.
3.   [Remove first node from AVAIL list.]
      Set NEW: = AVAIL and AVAIL: = LINK [AVAIL].
4.   Set INFO [NEW]: = ITEM.   [Copies new data into new node.]
5.   If LOC = NULL, then: [Insert as first node.]
            Set LINK [NEW]: = START and START: = NEW.
      Else: [Insert after node with location LOC.]
            Set LINK [NEW]: = LINK [LOC] and LINK [LOC]: = NEW.
      [End of If structure.]
6.   Exit.

FIND (START, INFO, LINK, ITEM, LOC)

This procedure finds the location LOC of the last node in a sorted list such that INFO [LOC] < ITEM, or sets LOC: = NULL.

1.   [List empty?]
      If START = NULL, then: Set LOC: = NULL, and Exit.
2.   [Special case?]
      If ITEM < INFO [START], then: Set LOC: = NULL, and Exit.
3.   Set SAVE: = START and PTR: = LINK [START].
      [Initializes pointers.]

4.   Repeat Steps 5 and 6 While PTR ≠ NULL.
5.   If ITEM < INFO [PTR], then:
                        Set LOC: = SAVE, and Exit.
                [End of If structure.]
6.   Set SAVE: = PTR and PTR: = LINK [PTR].   [Updates pointers.]
        [End of Step 4 loop.]
7.   Set LOC: = SAVE.
8.   Exit.

DELNODE (START, INFO, LINK, AVAIL, ITEM)

This algorithm deletes from a linked list the first node N that contains the given ITEM of information.

1.   Call FIND (START, INFO, LINK, ITEM, LOC, LOCP)
2.   If LOC = NULL, then: Write: ITEM not in list, and Exit.
3.   [Delete node.]
        If LOCP = NULL, then:
                Set START: = LINK [START].   [Deletes first node.]
        Else:
                Set LINK [LOCP] := LINK[LOC].
        [End of If structure.]
4.   [Return deleted node to the AVAIL list.]
        Set LINK [LOC]: = AVAIL and AVAIL: = LOC.
5.   Exit.

FIND (START, INFO, LINK, ITEM, LOC, LOCP)

        This procedure finds the location LOC of the first node N that contains ITEM and the location LOCP of the node preceding N. If ITEM does not appear in the list, then the procedure sets LOC =NULL; and if ITEM appears in the first node, then it sets LOCP = NULL.

1.   [List empty?]
        If START = NULL, then:
                Set LOC: = NULL and LOCP: = NULL, and Exit.
        [End of If structure.]
2.   [ITEM IN FIRST NODE?]
        If INFO [START] = ITEM, then:
                Set LOC: = START and LOCP: = NULL and Exit.
        [End of If structure.]
3.   Set SAVE: = START and PTR: = LINK [START]. [Initialize pointers.]
4.   Repeat Steps 5 and 6 While PTR ≠ NULL:
5.   If INFO [PTR]: = ITEM, then:
                        Set LOC: = PTR, LOCP: = SAVE and Exit.
                [End of If structure.]

6.   Set SAVE: = PTR and PTR: = LINK [PTR]   [Update Pointer.]
        [End of Step 4 Loop].
7.   Set LOC = NULL.   [Search Unsuccessful].
8.   Exit.

REVERSE (START, LINK)

This procedure reverses a link list.

1.   Set P3: = START, P2 = NULL.
2.   Repeat Steps 3 to 6, While P3 ≠ NULL:
3.   Set P1: = P2.
4.   Set P2: = P3.
5.   Set P3: = LINK [P3].
6.   Set LINK [P2]: = P1.
        [End of step 2 loop.]
7.   Set START: = P2.
8.   Exit.

SORT (INFO, LINK, START)

This procedure sorts a list using the selection sorting technique.
1.   Set P1: = START.
2.   Repeat Steps 3 to 5 while P1 ≠ NULL:
3.   Set P2: = LINK [P1].
4.   Repeat Step While P2 ≠ NULL:
                        If INFO [P1] > INFO [P2] , then:
                                (a) Set T: = INFO [P1].
                                (b) Set INFO [P1]: = INFO [P2].
                                (c) Set INFO [P2]: = T.
                        [End of If Structure.]
                        Set P2: = LINK [P2].
                [End of Step 4 loop.]
5.   Set P1: = LINK [P1].
        [End of step 2 loop.]
6.   Exit.

(STACK USING LINKED LIST)

PUSH (TOP, AVAIL, LINK, INFO, ITEM)
This procedure adds a new element at the TOP of a STACK using the link list.

1.   [OVERFLOW?]
        If AVAIL = NULL, then: Write: OVERFLOW and EXIT.
2.   [Remove the first node from AVAIL list.]
        Set NEW: = AVAIL, AVAIL : = LINK [AVAIL].
3.   Set INFO [NEW]: = ITEM.
4.   Set LINK [NEW]: =TOP.
5.   Set TOP: = NEW.
6.   Exit

POP (TOP, LINK, INFO, ITEM)

This procedure removes the element form the TOP of a stack using the link list.
1.   [UNDERFLOW?]
        If TOP = NULL, then: write: UNDERFLOW and Exit.
2.   Set PTR: =TOP.
3.   Set TOP: = LINK [TOP].
4.   Set ITEM: = INFO [PTR].
5.   Set LINK [PTR]: = AVAIL.
6.   Set AVAIL: = PTR.
7.   Exit

(QUEUE USING LINKED LIST)

ADDQ (FRONT, REAR, AVAIL, LINK, INFO, ITEM)

This procedure adds a new element in the REAR of a QUEUE using the link list.
1.   [OVERFLOW?]
        If AVAIL = NULL, then: Write: OVERFLOW and Exit.
2.   Set NEW: = AVAIL, AVAIL: = LINK [AVAIL].
3.   Set INFO [NEW]: = ITEM, LINK [NEW]: = NULL.
4.   If REAR: = NULL, then:
                Set FRONT: = NEW, REAR: = NEW.
5.   Else:
                Set LINK [REAR]: = NEW.
                Set REAR: = NEW.
        [End of If structure.]
6.   Exit.

DELQ (FRONT, REAR, LINK, INFO, ITEM)

This procedure removes the FRONT element of a QUEUE using the linked list.

1.   [UNDERFLOW?]
        If REAR = NULL, then: Write: UNDERFLOW and Exit.
2.   Set PTR: = FRONT.
3.   If FRONT = REAR Then

Set FRONT: = NULL, REAR: = NULL.
4.   Else:
                Set FRONT: = LINK [FRONT].
        [End of If Structure]
5.   Set ITEM: = INFO [PTR].
6.   Set LINK [PTR]: =AVAIL.
7.   Set AVAIL: = PTR.
8.   Exit.

Merge (L1, L2, L3, LINK, INFO, AVAIL).

This procedure merges two linked list L1 & L2 in L3.

1.   Set L3: = NULL.
2.   Repeat Step 3 While L1 ≠ NULL and L2 ≠ NULL:
3.   If INFO [L1] < INFO [L2], then:
                        Call APPEND (L3, LINK, INFO, AVAIL, INFO [L1]).
                        Set L1: = LINK [L1].
                Else:
                        Call APPEND (L3, LINK, INFO, AVAIL, INFO [L2]).
                        Set L2: = LINK [L2].
                [End of If Structure.]
        [End of Step 2 Loop].
4.   [Remaining of First list]
        Repeat steps while L1≠ NULL:
                Call APPEND (L3, LINK, INFO, AVAIL, INFO [L2]).
                Set L1: = LINK [L1].
        [End of Step 4 Loop].
5.   [Remaining of Second list]
        Repeat Steps While L2 ≠ NULL:
                Call APPEND (L3, LINK, INFO, AVAIL, INFO[L2]).
                Set L2: = LINK [L2]
        [End of Step 5 Loop].
6.   Exit.

ADD_POLY (L1, L2, L3, LINK, COEFF, POW, AVAIL)

This procedure adds two polynomial equations L1 & L2 and assign the sum in L3.

1.   Set L3: = NULL.
2.   Repeat Step 3 While L1 ≠ NULL and L2 ≠ NULL:
3.   If POW [L1] = POW [L2], then:
                Call APPEND (L3, LINK,COEFF ,POW ,
        AVAIL,COEFF[L1]+COEFF[L2], POW[L1])
                    Set L1: = LINK [L1].
                    Set L2: = LINK [L2].

Else If POW [L1] > POW [L2], then:

    Call APPEND (L3, LINK, COEFF, POW, AVAIL, COEFF[L1], POW[L1]).

        Set L1: = LINK [L1].

  Else:

    Call APPEND (L3, LINK, COEFF, POW, AVAIL, COEFF[L2], POW[L2]).

        Set L2: = LINK [L2].

  [End of If Structure.]

  [End of step 2 loop.]

4.   [Remaining of first list.]

Repeat steps while L1 ≠ NULL:

    Call APPEND (L3, LINK, COEFF, POW, AVAIL, COEFF[L1], POW[L1].

        Set L1: = LINK [L1].

  [End of step 4 loop.]

5.   [Remaining of second list]

Repeat steps while L2 ≠ NULL:

    Call APPEND (L3, LINK, COEFF, POW, AVAIL, COEFF[L2], POW[L2].

        Set L2: = LINK [L2].

  [End of step 5 loop.]

6.   Exit.

Doubly Linked List-

In a doubly linked list, also called two-way list, each node is divided into three parts:

- The first part, called BACK pointer field, contains the address of the preceding element in the list,

- The second part contains the information of the element, and

- The third part, called FORW pointer field, contains the address of the succeeding element in the list.

In addition, two pointer variables, for example FIRST and LAST, are used that contains the address of the first element and the address of the last element of the list, respectively.

The first node contains NULL value in the BACK pointer field to indicate there is no element preceding it in the list, and the last element have NULL value in the FORW pointer field to indicate that there is no element succeeding it in the list. Doubly linked lists can be traverse in both directions.

TRAVERSE (FIRST, INFO, FORW)

Let LIST be a linked list in the memory. This algorithm traverses LIST, applying an operation PROCESS to each element of the LIST. The variable PTR points to the node currently being processed.

1.   Set PTR: = FIRST.   [Initializes pointer PTR.]
2.   Repeat Steps 3 and 4 While PTR ≠ NULL:
3.   Apply PROCESS to INFO [PTR].
4.   Set PTR: = FORW [PTR].   [PTR now points to the next node.]
      [End of Step 2 loop.]
5.   Exit.

REVERSE_TRAVERSE (LAST, INFO, BACK)

Let LIST be a linked list in the memory. This algorithm traverses LIST from Right to Left, applying an operation PROCESS to each element of the LIST. The variable PTR points to the node currently being processed.

1.   Set PTR: = LAST.   [Initializes pointer PTR.]
2.   Repeat Steps 3 and 4 While PTR ≠ NULL:
3.   Apply PROCESS to INFO [PTR].
4.   Set PTR: =BACK [PTR].   [PTR now points to the next node.]
      [End of step 2 loop.]
5.   Exit.

COUNT (FIRST, INFO, FORW, CNT)

Let LIST be a linked list in the memory. This algorithm counts the number of nodes in the LIST and stores the result in CNT.

1.   Set CNT: = 0.   [Initialize counter.]
2.   Set PTR: = FIRST.   [Initializes pointer PTR.]
3.   Repeat Step 4 and 5 while PTR ≠ NULL:
4   Set CNT: = CNT + 1.   [Increment counter by 1.]
5.   Set PTR: = FORW [PTR]. [PTR now points to the next node.]
      [End of step 2 loop.]
6.   Exit.

SEARCH (FIRST, INFO, FORW, ITEM, LOC)

LIST is a linked list in memory. This algorithm finds the location LOC of the node where ITEM first appears in LIST, or sets LOC: = NULL.

1.   Set PTR: =FIRST.
2.   Repeat Step 3 While PTR ≠ NULL:
3.   If ITEM = INFO [PTR], then:
                        Set LOC: =PTR, and Exit.
               Else:
                        Set PTR: = FORW [PTR].
               [End of If structure.]
       [End of Step 2 loop.]
4.   [Search is unsuccessful.]
       Set LOC: = NULL.
5.   Exit.

ADDFIRST (FIRST, LAST, INFO, BACK, FORW, AVAIL, ITEM)

This procedure adds a new node at the beginning of a two-way linked list.

1.   [OVERFLOW?]
       If AVAIL = NULL, then: Write: OVERFLOW and Exit.
2.   [Remove the first node from AVAIL list.]
       Set NEW: = AVAIL, AVAIL: = FORW [AVAIL].
3.   Set INFO [NEW]: = ITEM.   [Copies new data into new node.]
4.   Set BACK [NEW]: = NULL.
5.   If FIRST = NULL, then: [If we are adding first ITEM in the list.]
                Set FIRST: = NEW, LAST: = NEW.
                Set FORW [NEW] : = NULL.
       Else:
                Set FORW [NEW]: = FIRST.   [New node now points to
       original first node.]
                Set BACK [FIRST]: = NEW.
                Set FIRST: = NEW.   [Changes FIRST so it points
       to the new node.]
       [End of If structure.]
6.   Exit.

APPEND (FIRST, LAST, INFO, BACK, FORW, ITEM, AVAIL)

This procedure adds a new node at the end of a two-way linked list.

1.   [OVERFLOW?]
       If AVAIL = NULL, then: Write: OVERFLOW and Exit.
2.   [Remove the first node from AVAIL list.]
       Set NEW: = AVAIL, AVAIL: = FORW [AVAIL].
3.   Set INFO [NEW]: = ITEM.   [Copies new data into new node.]
4.   Set FORW [NEW]: = NULL.
5.   If FIRST = NULL, then: [If we are adding first ITEM in the list.]
                Set FIRST: =NEW, LAST: = NEW.

Set BACK [NEW]: = NULL.
Else:
        Set FORW [LAST]: = NEW.
Set BACK [NEW]: = LAST. [New node now points to original first node.]
Set LAST: = NEW.   [Changes LAST so it points to the new node.]
       [End of If structure.]
6.   Exit.

ADDAFTER (FIRST, LAST, LINK, INFO, AVAIL, ITEM, POS)

This procedure adds a new elements after the given position pos.

1.   Set PTR: = FIRST.
2.   Repeat steps For I: = 1 to POS – 1:
           Set PTR: = FORW [PTR].
       If PTR = NULL, then: Write "Such a node does not exit " and Exit.
       [End of step 2 loop.]
3.   [OVERFLOW?]
       If AVAIL = NULL, then: Write: OVERFLOW and Exit.
4.   [Remove the first node from AVAIL list.]
       Set NEW: = AVAIL, AVAIL: = FORW [AVAIL].
5.   Set INFO [NEW]: = ITEM.   [Copies new data into new node.]
6.   Set FORW [NEW]: = FORW [PTR], BACK [FORW [PTR]]: = NEW.
7.   Set BACK [NEW]: = PTR, FORW [PTR]: = NEW.
8.   Exit.

INSLOC (FIRST, LAST, INFO, BACK, FORW, AVAIL, ITEM)

This algorithm inserts ITEM into a sorted linked list.

1.   Call FIND (INFO, FORW, FIRST, ITEM, LOC).
2.   [OVERFLOW?]
       If AVAIL = NULL, then: Write: OVERFLOW, and Exit.
3.   [Remove first node from AVAIL list.]
       Set NEW: =AVAIL and AVAIL: = FORW [AVAIL].
4.   Set INFO [NEW]: = ITEM.   [Copies new data into new node.]
5.   If LOC = NULL, then: [Insert as first node.]
           If LAST = NULL, then Set LAST: = NEW.
           Set FORW [NEW]: = FIRST.
           Set BACK [FIRST]: = NEW.
           Set FIRST: = NEW.
      Else: [Insert after node with location LOC.]
           Set FORW [NEW]: = FORW [LOC]
           If FORW [LOC] ≠ NULL, then: BACK [FORW [LOC]]: = NEW.
           FORW [LOC]: = NEW.
           BACK [NEW]: = LOC.

If LAST = LOC, then: LAST: = NEW.
[End of If structure.]
6.   Exit.

FIND (FIRST, ITEM, INFO, FORW, LOC)

This procedure finds the location LOC of the last node in a sorted list such that INFO [LOC] < ITEM, or sets LOC = NULL.

1.   [List empty?]
        If FIRST = NULL, then: Set LOC: = NULL, and Exit.
2.   [Special case?]
        If ITEM < INFO [START], then: Set LOC: = NULL, and Exit.
3.   Set SAVE: =FIRST and PTR: = FORW [START].
        [Initializes pointers.]
4.   Repeat Steps 5 and 6 While PTR $\neq$ NULL:
5.   If ITEM < INFO [PTR], then:
                      Set LOC: =SAVE, and Exit.
              [End of If structure.]
6.   Set SAVE: = PTR and PTR: = FORW [PTR]. [Updates pointers.]
        [End of Step 4 loop.]
7.   Set LOC: = SAVE.
8.   Exit.

DELNODE (FIRST, LAST, INFO, BACK, FORW, AVAIL, ITEM)
This algorithm deletes from a linked list the first node N that contains the given ITEM of information.

1.   Call FIND (FIRST, LAST, INFO, BACK, FORW, ITEM, LOC, LOCP)
2.   If LOC = NULL, then: Write: ITEM not in list, and Exit.
3.   [Delete node.]
        If LOCP = NULL, then:
              If FIRST = LAST, then:
                      Set FIRST: = NULL, LAST: = NULL.
              Else:
                      Set FIRST: = FORW [FIRST]. [Deletes first node.]
                      Set BACK [FIRST]: = NULL.
              [End of If Structure.]
        Else:
              IF FORW [LOC] $\neq$ NULL, then: BACK [FORW [LOC]]: = LOCP.
              Set FORW [LOCP]: = FORW [LOC].
              If LAST = LOC, then: Set LAST: = BACK [LOC].
        [End of If structure.]
4.   [Return deleted node to the AVAIL list.]
        Set FORW [LOC]: = AVAIL and AVAIL: = LOC.
5.   Exit.

FIND (FIRST, INFO, FORW, ITEM, LOC, LOCP)

This procedure finds the location LOC of the first node N which contains ITEM and the location LOCP of the node preceding N. If ITEM does not appear in the list, then the procedure sets LOC:= NULL; and if ITEM appears in the first node, then it sets LOCP = NULL.

1.   [List empty?]
        If FIRST =NULL, then:
                Set LOC: = NULL and LOCP: = NULL, and Exit.
        [End of If structure.]
2.   [ITEM IN FIRST NODE?]
        If INFO [FIRST] = ITEM, then:
                Set LOC: = START and LOCP: = NULL and Exit.
        [End of If structure.]
3.   Set SAVE: = FIRST and PTR: = LINK [FIRST]. [Initialize pointers.]
4.   Repeat Steps 5 and 6 While PTR ≠ NULL:
5.   If INFO [PTR]: = ITEM, then:
                        Set LOC: = PTR, LOCP: = SAVE and Exit.
                [End of If structure.]
6.   Set SAVE: = PTR and PTR: = FORW [PTR] [Update Pointer.]
        [End of Step 4 Loop].
7.   Set LOC = NULL. [Search Unsuccessful.]
8.   Exit.

Circular Header Linked List-

A circular header list is linked list which always contains a special node, called header node, at the beginning of the linked list. This header node usually contains vital information about the linked list such as the number of nodes in the lists, whether the list is sorted or not, etc. In circular header list the last node contains the address of header in its FORW field.

TRAVERSE (START, INFO, LINK)

This procedure traverses the circular header link list.

1.   Set PTR: =LINK [START].
2.   Repeat Steps 3 to 4 While PTR ≠ START:
3.   Apply a PROCESS on INFO [PTR].
4.   Set PTR: =: LINK [PTR].
        [End of Step 3 Loop.]
5.   Exit.

COUNT (START, INFO, LINK, CNT)

Let LIST be a linked list in the memory. This algorithm counts the number of nodes in the LIST and stores the result in CNT.

1.	Set CNT: = 0.	[Initialize counter.]
2.	Set PTR: = LINK[START].	[Initializes pointer PTR.]
3.	Repeat Steps 4 and 5 While PTR ≠ START:	
4	Set CNT: = CNT + 1.	[Increment counter by 1.]
5.	Set PTR: = LINK [PTR].	[PTR now points to the next node.]
	[End of step 2 loop.]	
1.	Exit.	

SEARCH (START, INFO, LINK, ITEM, LOC)

LIST is a linked list in memory. This algorithm finds the location LOC of the node where ITEM first appears in LIST, or sets LOC: = NULL.

1.   Set PTR: = LINK [START].
2.   Repeat Step 3 While PTR ≠ START:
3.   If ITEM = INFO [PTR], then:
                        Set LOC: =PTR, and Exit.
        Else:
                        Set PTR: = LINK [PTR].
                [End of If Structure.]
        [End of Step 2 loop.]
4.   [Search is unsuccessful.]
        Set LOC: = NULL.
5.   Exit.

SRCHSL (START, INFO, LINK, ITEM, LOC)

LIST is a sorted list in the memory. This algorithm finds the location LOC of the node where ITEM first appears in LIST, or sets LOC: = NULL.

1.   Set PTR: = LINK [START].
2.   Repeat step 3 While PTR ≠ START:
3.   If ITEM > INFO [PTR], then:
                        Set PTR: = LINK [PTR].   [PTR now points to the next node.]
                Else If ITEM = INFO [PTR], then:
                        Set LOC: =PTR, and Exit. [Search is successful]
                Else:
                        Set LOC: =NULL, and Exit.   [ITEM now exceeds INFO [PTR].]

[End of If structure.]
[End of Step 2 loop.]
4.   Set LOC: =NULL.
5.   Exit.

ADDFIRST (START, INFO, LINK, ITEM, AVAIL)

This procedure adds a new node at the beginning of list.

1.   [OVERFLOW?]
        If AVAIL = NULL, then: Write: OVERFLOW and Exit.
2.   [Remove the first node from AVAIL list.]
        Set NEW: = AVAIL, AVAIL: = LINK [AVAIL].
3.   Set INFO [NEW]: = ITEM.   [Copies new data into new node.]
4.   If LINK [START] = START, then:
                Set LINK [START]: = NEW.
                Set LINK [NEW]: = START.
        Else:
                Set LINK [NEW]: = LINK [START].
                Set LINK [START]: = NEW.
        [End of If structure.]
5.   Exit.

APPEND (START, INFO, LINK, AVAIL, ITEM)

This procedure adds a new element at the end of LIST.

1.   [OVERFLOW?]
        If AVAIL = NULL, then: Write: OVERFLOW and Exit.
2.   [Remove the first node from AVAIL list.]
        Set NEW: = AVAIL, AVAIL: = LINK [AVAIL].
3.   Set INFO [NEW]: = ITEM.   [Copies new data into new node.]
4.   If LINK [START] = START, then:
                Set LINK [START]: = NEW.
        Else:
                Set PTR: = LINK [START].   [Initialize pointer.]
                Repeat Step While LINK [PTR] $\neq$ START:
                        Set PTR: = LINK [PTR].
                [End of loop]
                Set LINK [PTR]: = NEW.
        [End of If structure.]
5.   LINK [NEW]: = START.
6.   Exit.

ADDAFTER (START, LINK, INFO, AVAIL, ITEM, POS)

This procedure adds a new elements after the given position pos.

1.   Set PTR: = LINK [START].
2.   Repeat steps For I: = 1 to POS – 1:
                Set PTR: = LINK [PTR].
      If PTR = START then: Write "Such a node does not exit " and Exit
      [End of step 2 loop.]
3.   [OVERFLOW?]
      If AVAIL = NULL, then: Write: OVERFLOW and Exit.
4.   [Remove the first node from AVAIL list.]
      Set NEW: = AVAIL, AVAIL: = LINK [AVAIL].
5.   Set INFO [NEW]: = ITEM.   [Copies new data into new node.]
6.   Set LINK [NEW]: = LINK [PTR].
7.   Set LINK [PTR]: = NEW.
8.   Exit.

INSLOC (START, INFO, LINK, AVAIL, ITEM)

This algorithm inserts ITEM into a sorted linked list.

1.   Call FIND (START, INFO, LINK, ITEM, LOC).
2.   [OVERFLOW?]
      If AVAIL = NULL, then: Write: OVERFLOW, and Exit.
3.   [Remove first node from AVAIL list.]
      Set NEW: =AVAIL and AVAIL: = LINK [AVAIL].
4.   Set INFO [NEW]: = ITEM.   [Copies new data into new node.]
5.   If LOC = NULL, then: [Insert as first node.]
                Set LINK [NEW]: = LINK [START] and Link [START]: = NEW.
      Else: [Insert after node with location LOC.]
                Set LINK [NEW]: = LINK [LOC] and LINK [LOC]: = NEW.
      [End of If structure.]
6.   Exit.

FIND (START, INFO, LINK, ITEM, LOC)

This procedure finds the location LOC of the last node in a sorted list such that
INFO [LOC] < ITEM, or sets LOC: = NULL.
1.   [List empty?]
      If LINK [START] = NULL, then: Set LOC: =NULL, and Exit.
2.   [Special case?]
      If ITEM <INFO [LINK [START]], then: Set LOC: = NULL, and Exit.
3.   Set SAVE: =LINK [START] and PTR: = LINK [LINK [START]].
      [Initializes pointers.]

4.   Repeat Steps 5 and 6 while PTR ≠ START.
5.   If ITEM < INFO [PTR], then:
                  Set LOC: =SAVE, and Exit.
            [End of If structure.]
6.   Set SAVE: = PTR and PTR: = LINK [PTR]. [Updates pointers.]
      [End of Step 4 loop.]
7.   Set LOC: = SAVE.
8.   Exit.

DELNODE (START, INFO, LINK, AVAIL, ITEM)

This algorithm deletes from a linked list the first node N that contains the given ITEM of information.

1.   Call FIND (START, INFO, LINK, ITEM, LOC, LOCP)
2.   If LOC = NULL, then: Write: ITEM not in list, and Exit.
3.   [Delete node.]
      If LOCP = NULL, then:
      Set LINK [START]: = LINK [LINK [START]]. [Deletes first node.]
      Else:
            Set LINK [LOCP]: = LINK [LOC].
      [End of If structure.]
4.   [Return deleted node to the AVAIL list.]
      Set LINK [LOC]: = AVAIL and AVAIL := LOC.
5.   Exit.

FIND (START, INFO, LINK, ITEM, LOC, LOCP)

      This procedure finds the location LOC of the first node N which contains ITEM and the location LOCP of the node preceding N. If ITEM does not appear in the list, then the procedure sets LOC =NULL; and if ITEM appears in the first node, then it sets LOCP: = NULL.

1.   [List empty?]
      If LINK [START] =NULL, then
            Set LOC: = NULL and LOCP: = NULL, and Exit.
      [End of If structure.]
2.   [ITEM IN FIRST NODE?]
      If INFO [LINK [START]] = ITEM, then:
            Set LOC: = LINK [START] and LOCP: =NULL and Exit.
      [End of If structure.]
2.   Set SAVE: = LINK [START] and PTR: = LINK[LINK[START]].
      [Initialize pointers.]
4.   Repeat Step 5 and 6 while PTR ≠ START:
5.   If INFO [PTR]: = ITEM, then:
                  Set LOC: = PTR, LOCP: = SAVE and Exit.
            [End of If structure.]
6.   Set SAVE: = PTR and PTR: = LINK [PTR] [Update Pointer.]
      [End of Step 4 Loop].
7.   Set LOC: = NULL. [Search unsuccessful].
8.   Exit.

/*Singly linklist */

```
1.      #include<stdio.h>
2.      #include<conio.h>
3.      #include<alloc.h>
4.      struct node
5.      {
6.              int info;
7.              struct node * link;
8.      };
9.      struct node * getnode();
10.     void addfirst(struct node **, int);
11.     void append(struct node**, int);
12.     void addafter(struct node**, int,int);
13.     void insert_in_sortedlist(struct node **, int);
14.     void delnode(struct node**, int);
15.     void traverse(struct node *);
16.     int count(struct node *);
17.     void freeall(struct node**);
18.     void search(struct node*,int, struct node**,struct node**);
19.     void sort(struct node*);
20.     void reverse(struct node**);
21.     void find(struct node * , int, struct node **);
22.     void main()
23.     {
24.             struct node *p;
25.             int item,pos,cnt,ch;
26.             p = NULL;
27.             do
28.             {
29.                     clrscr();
30.             printf("1. Addfirst\n2. Append\n3. Addafter\n4. delete\n \
31.             5. Traverse\n6. Count\n7. sort\n8. reverse\n9. Insert\n \
32.             10. exit\n");
33.                     printf("enter your choice");
34.                     scanf("%d",&ch);
35.                     switch(ch)
36.                     {
37.                             case 1:
38.                                     printf("Enter a number");
39.                                     scanf("%d",&item);
40.                                     addfirst(&p,item);
41.                                     break;
```

```
42.                           case 2:
43.                                   printf("Enter a number");
44.                                   scanf("%d",&item);
45.                                   append(&p,item);
46.                                   break;
47.                           case 3:
48.                                   printf("Enter a number and pos");
49.                                   scanf("%d%d",&item,&pos);
50.                                   addafter(&p,item,pos);
51.                                   break;
52.                           case 4:
53.                                   printf("Enter item to delete");
54.                                   scanf("%d",&item);
55.                                   delnode(&p,item);
56.                                   break;
57.                           case 5:
58.                                   traverse(p);
59.                                   break;
60.                           case 6:
61.                                   cnt = count(p);
62.                                   printf("%d",cnt);
63.                                   break;
64.                           case 7:
65.                                   sort(p);
66.                                   break;
67.                           case 8:
68.                                   reverse(&p);
69.                                   break;
70.                           case 9:
71.                                   printf("Enter item to insert");
72.                                   scanf("%d",&item);
73.                                   insert_in_sortedlist(&p,item);
74.                                   break;
75.                           case 10:
76.                                   freeall(&p);
77.                                   break;
78.                           default:
79.                                   printf("Invalid choice");
80.                   }
81.               getch();
82.           }while(ch != 10);
83.       }
84.       struct node * getnode()
85.       {
86.               struct node * t;
87.               t = (struct node *)malloc(sizeof(struct node));
```

```c
88.              return (t);
89.      }
90.      void addfirst(struct node** start, int item)
91.      {
92.              struct node *new;
93.              new = getnode();
94.              if(new == NULL)
95.              {
96.                      printf("Overflow");
97.                      return;
98.              }
99.              new->info = item;
100.             new->link = *start;
101.             *start = new;
102.     }
103.     void append(struct node ** start, int item)
104.     {
105.             struct node* new,*ptr;
106.             new = getnode();
107.             if(new == NULL)
108.             {
109.                     printf("Overflow");
110.                     return;
111.             }
112.             new->info = item;
113.             new->link = NULL;
114.             if(*start == NULL)
115.                     *start = new;
116.             else
117.             {
118.                     ptr = *start;
119.                     while(ptr->link != NULL)
120.                             ptr = ptr->link;
121.                     ptr->link = new;
122.             }
123.     }
124.     void traverse(struct node *start)
125.     {
126.             struct node *ptr;
127.             ptr = start;
128.             while(ptr != NULL)
129.             {
130.                     printf("%d\t",ptr->info);
131.                     ptr = ptr->link;
132.             }
133.     }
```

```c
134.    int count(struct node *start)
135.    {
136.            struct node *ptr;
137.            int cnt = 0;
138.            ptr = start;
139.            while(ptr != NULL)
140.            {
141.            cnt++;
142.            ptr = ptr->link;
143.            }
144.            return (cnt);
145.    }
146.    void freeall(struct node **start)
147.    {
148.            struct node *ptr;
149.            while(*start != NULL)
150.            {
151.                    ptr = *start;
152.                    *start = (*start)->link;
153.                    free(ptr);
154.            }
155.    }
156.    void search(struct node* start, int item, struct node** loc, struct node** locp)
157.    {
158.            struct node *save,*ptr;
159.    if(start == NULL)
160.            {
161.                    *loc = *locp = NULL;
162.                    return;
163.            }
164.            if(item == start->info)
165.            {
166.                    *loc = start;
167.                    *locp = NULL;
168.                    return;
169.            }
170.            save = start;
171.            ptr = start->link;
172.            while(ptr != NULL)
173.            {
174.                    if(ptr->info == item)
175.                    {
176.                            *loc = ptr;
177.                            *locp = save;
178.                            return;
179.                    }
```

```
180.                         save = ptr;
181.                         ptr=ptr->link;
182.                 }
183.                 *loc = *locp = NULL;
184.         }
185.     /* or
186.     void search(struct node* start, int item, struct node** loc, struct node** locp)
187.     {
188.                 *locp = NULL;
189.                 *loc = start;
190.                 while(*loc != NULL && (*loc)->info != item)
191.                 {
192.                         *locp = *loc;
193.                         *loc = (*loc)->link;
194.                 }
195.     }
196.     */
197.     void delnode(struct node** start, int item)
198.     {
199.                 struct node *loc,*locp;
200.                 search(*start,item,&loc,&locp);
201.                 if(loc == NULL)
202.                         printf("Item not in the list");
203.                 else if(locp == NULL)
204.                         *start = (*start)->link;
205.                 else
206.                         locp->link = loc->link;
207.     free(loc);
208.     }
209.     void sort(struct node* start)
210.     {
211.                 struct node *p1,*p2;
212.                 int t;
213.                 for(p1=start;p1->link != NULL;p1 = p1->link)
214.                         for(p2= p1->link; p2 != NULL; p2= p2->link)
215.                                 if(p1->info > p2->info)
216.                                 {
217.                                         t = p1->info;
219.                                         p1->info = p2->info;
220.                                         p2->info = t;
221.                                 }
222.     }
223.     void reverse(struct node ** start)
224.     {
225.                 struct node *p1,*p2,*p3;
226.                 p3 = *start;
```

```
227.            p2 = NULL;
228.            while(p3!=NULL)
229.            {
230.                    p1 = p2;
231.                    p2 = p3;
232.                    p3=p3->link;
234.                    p2->link = p1;
235.            }
236.            *start = p2;
237.    }
238.    void addafter(struct node** start, int item, int pos)
239.    {
240.            struct node* new,*ptr;
241.            int i;
242.            for(ptr = *start, i = 1; i<pos; i++,ptr = ptr->link)
243.            {
244.                    if(ptr == NULL)
245.                    {
246.                            printf("Such a node does not exist");
247.                            return;
248.                    }
249.            }
250.            new = getnode();
251.            if(new == NULL)
252.            {
253.                    printf("Overflow");
254.                    return;
255.            }
256.            new->info = item;
257.            new->link = ptr->link;
258.            ptr->link = new;
259.    }
260.    void find(struct node * start, int item, struct node ** loc)
261.    {
262.            struct node *save, *ptr;
263.    if(start == NULL || item < start->info)
264.            {
265.                    *loc = NULL;
266.                    return;
267.            }
268.            save = start;
269.            ptr = start->link;
270.            while(ptr !=NULL)
271.            {
272.                    if(item < ptr->info)
273.                    {
```

```
274.                              *loc = save;
275.                              return;
276.                    }
277.                    save = ptr;
278.                    ptr = ptr->link;
279.          }
280.          *loc = save;
281.    }
282.    void insert_in_sortedlist(struct node **start, int item)
283.    {
284.          struct node *new,*ptr,*loc;
285.          find(*start,item,&loc);
286.          new = getnode();
287.          if(new == NULL)
288.          {
289.                    printf("Overflow");
290.                    return ;
291.          }
292.          new->info = item;
292.          if(loc == NULL)
293.          {
294.                    new->link = *start;
295.                    *start = new;
296.          }
297.          else
298.          {
299.                    new->link = loc->link;
300.                    loc->link = new;
301.          }
302.    }
```

/*Doubly linklist */
```
1.      #include<stdio.h>
2.      #include<conio.h>
3.      #include<alloc.h>
4.      struct node
5.      {
6.              int info;
7.              struct node * back,*forw;
8.      };
9.      struct node * getnode();
10.     void addfirst(struct node **,struct node ** , int);
11.     void append(struct node**,struct node **, int);
12.     void ad1dafter(struct node**,struct node **, int,int);
13.     void insert_in_sortedlist(struct node **,struct node **, int);
14.     void delnode(struct node**,struct node **, int);
```

```
15.     void traverse(struct node *);
16.     void traverse2(struct node *);
17.     int count(struct node *);
18.     void freeall(struct node**,struct node**);
19.     void search(struct node*,int, struct node**,struct node**);
20.     void sort(struct node*);
21.     void find(struct node * , int, struct node **);
22.     void main()
23.     {
24.             struct node *p1,*p2;
25.             int item,pos,cnt,ch;
26.             p1 = p2 = NULL;
27.             do
26.             {
27.                     clrscr();
28.     printf("1. Addfirst\n2. Append\n3. Addafter\n4. delete\n \
29.     5. Traverse\n6. Traverse rev.\n7. Count\n8. sort\n9. Insert\n \
30.     10. exit\n");
31.                     printf("enter your choice");
32.                     scanf("%d",&ch);
33.                     switch(ch)
34.                     {
35.                             case 1:
36.                                     printf("Enter a number");
37.                                     scanf("%d",&item);
38.                                     addfirst(&p1,&p2,item);
39.                                     break;
40.                             case 2:
41.                                     printf("Enter a number");
42.                                     scanf("%d",&item);
43.                                     append(&p1,&p2,item);
44.                                     break;
45.                             case 3:
46.                                     printf("Enter a number and pos");
47.                                     scanf("%d%d",&item,&pos);
48.                                     addafter(&p1,&p2,item,pos);
49.                                     break;
50.                             case 4:
51.                                     printf("Enter item to delete");
52.                                     scanf("%d",&item);
53.                                     delnode(&p1,&p2,item);
54.                                     break;
55.                             case 5:
56.                                     traverse(p1);
57.                                     break;
58.                             case 6:
```

```
59.                          traverse2(p2);
60.                          break;
61.                  case 7:
62.                          cnt = count(p1);
63.                          printf("%d",cnt);
64.                          break;
65.                  case 8:
66.                          sort(p1);
67.                          break;
68.                  case 9:
69.                          printf("Enter item to insert");
70.                          scanf("%d",&item);
71.                          insert_in_sortedlist(&p1,&p2,item);
72.                          break;
73.                  case 10:
74.                          freeall(&p1,&p2);
75.                          break;
76.                  default:
77.                          printf("Invalid choice");
78.              }
79.          getch();
80.      }while(ch != 10);
81.  }
82.  struct node * getnode()
83.  {
84.          struct node * t;
85.          t = (struct node *)malloc(sizeof(struct node));
86.          return (t);
87.  }
88.  void addfirst(struct node** first, struct node** last, int item)
89.  {
90.          struct node *new;
91.          new = getnode();
92.          if(new == NULL)
93.          {
94.                  printf("Overflow");
95.                  return;
96.          }
97.          new->info = item;
98.          new->back = NULL;
99.          if(*first == NULL)
100.         {
101.                 *first = *last = new;
102.                 new->forw = NULL;
103.         }
104.         else
```

```
105.              {
106.                      new->forw = *first;
107.                      (*first)->back = new;
108.                      *first = new;
109.              }
110.    }
111.    void append(struct node** first, struct node** last, int item)
112.    {
113.              struct node* new;
114.              new = getnode();
115.              if(new == NULL)
116.              {
117.                      printf("Overflow");
118.                      return;
119.              }
120.              new->info = item;
121.              new->forw = NULL;
122.              if(*first == NULL)
123.              {
124.                      *first = *last = new;
125.                      new->back = NULL;
126.              }
127.              else
128.              {
129.                      (*last)->forw = new;
130.                      new->back = *last;
131.                      *last = new;
132.              }
133.    }
134.    void traverse(struct node *first)
135.    {
136.              struct node *ptr;
137.              ptr = first;
138.              while(ptr != NULL)
139.              {
140.                      printf("%d\t",ptr->info);
141.                      ptr = ptr->forw;
142.              }
143.    }
144.    void traverse2(struct node *last)
145.    {
146.              struct node *ptr;
147.              ptr = last;
148.              while(ptr != NULL)
149.              {
150.                      printf("%d\t",ptr->info);
```

```
151.                    ptr = ptr->back;
152.            }
153.    }
154.    int count(struct node *first)
155.    {
156.            struct node *ptr;
157.            int cnt = 0;
158.            ptr = first;
159.            while(ptr != NULL)
160.            {
161.                    cnt++;
162.                    ptr = ptr->forw;
163.            }
164.            return (cnt);
165.    }
166.    void freeall(struct node** first, struct node** last)
167.    {
168.            struct node *ptr;
169.            while(*first != NULL)
170.            {
171.                    ptr = *first;
172.                    *first = (*first)->forw;
173.                    free(ptr);
174.            }
175.            *last = NULL;
176.    }
177.    void search(struct node* first, int item, struct node** loc, struct node** locp)
178.    {
179.            struct node *save,*ptr;
180.            if(first == NULL)
181.            {
182.                    *loc = *locp = NULL;
183.                    return;
184.            }
185.            if(item == first->info)
186.            {
187.                    *loc = first;
188.                    *locp = NULL;
189.                    return;
190.            }
191.            save = first;
192.            ptr = first->forw;
193.            while(ptr != NULL)
194.            {
195.                    if(ptr->info == item)
196.                    {
```

```
197.                              *loc = ptr;
198.                              *locp = save;
199.                              return;
200.                          }
201.                      save = ptr;
202.                      ptr=ptr->forw;
203.                  }
204.              *loc = *locp = NULL;
205.      }
206.      /* or
207.      void search(struct node* first, int item, struct node** loc, struct node** locp)
208.      {
209.              *locp = NULL;
210.              *loc = first;
211.              while(*loc != NULL && (*loc)->info != item)
212.              {
213.                      *locp = *loc;
214.                      *loc = (*loc)->forw;
215.              }
216.      }
217.      */
218.      void delnode(struct node** first, struct node** last, int item)
219.      {
220.              struct node *loc,*locp;
221.              search(*first,item,&loc,&locp);
222.              if(loc == NULL)
223.                      printf("Item not in the list");
224.              else if(locp == NULL)
225.              {
226.                      if(*first == *last)
227.                              *first = *last = NULL;
228.                      else
229.                      {
230.                              *first = (*first)->forw;
231.                              (*first)->back = NULL;
232.                      }
233.              }
234.              else
235.              {       if(loc->forw != NULL)
236.                              loc->forw->back = locp;
237.                      locp->forw = loc->forw;
238.                      if(*last == loc)
239.                              *last = loc->back;
240.              }
241.              free(loc);
242.      }
```

```
243.    void sort(struct node* first)
244.    {
245.            struct node *p1,*p2;
246.            int t;
247.            for(p1=first;p1->forw != NULL;p1 = p1->forw)
248.                    for(p2= p1->forw; p2 != NULL; p2= p2->forw)
249.                            if(p1->info > p2->info)
250.                            {
251.                                    t = p1->info;
252.                                    p1->info = p2->info;
253.                                    p2->info = t;
254.                            }
256.    }
257.    void addafter(struct node** first, struct node** last, int item, int pos)
258.    {
259.            struct node* new,*ptr;
260.            int i;
261.            for(ptr = *first, i = 1; i<pos; i++,ptr = ptr->forw)
262.            {
263.                    if(ptr == NULL)
264.                    {
265.                            printf("Such a node does not exist");
266.                            return;
267.                    }
268.            }
269.            new = getnode();
270.            if(new == NULL)
271.            {
272.                    printf("Overflow");
273.                    return;
274.            }
275.            new->info = item;
276.            new->forw = ptr->forw;
277.            if(ptr->forw != NULL)
278.                    ptr->forw->back = new;
279.            new->back = ptr;
280.            ptr->forw = new;
281.            if(*last == ptr)
282.                    *last = new;
283.    }
284.    void find(struct node * first, int item, struct node ** loc)
285.    {
286.            struct node *save, *ptr;
287.
288.            if(first == NULL || item < first->info)
289.            {
```

```
290.                    *loc = NULL;
291.                    return;
292.          }
293.          save = first;
294.          ptr = first->forw;
295.          while(ptr !=NULL)
296.          {
297.                  if(item < ptr->info)
298.                  {
299.                          *loc = save;
300.                          return;
301.                  }
302.                  save = ptr;
303.                  ptr = ptr->forw;
304.          }
305.          *loc = save;
306.   }
307.   void insert_in_sortedlist(struct node** first, struct node** last, int item)
308.   {
309.          struct node *new,*ptr,*loc;
310.          find(*first,item,&loc);
311.          new = getnode();
312.          if(new == NULL)
313.          {
314.                  printf("Overflow");
315.                  return ;
316.          }
317.          new->info = item;
318.          if(loc == NULL)
319.          {
320.                  if(*last == NULL)
321.                          *last = new;
322.                  new->forw = *first;
323.                  (*first)->back = new;
324.                  *first = new;
325.          }
326.          else
327.          {
328.                  new->forw = loc->forw;
329.                  if(loc->forw !=NULL)
330.                          loc->forw->back = new;
331.                  loc->forw = new;
332.                  new->back = loc;
333.                  if(*last == loc)
334.                          *last = new;
335.          } }
```

/*Circular Header linklist */

```
1.       #include<stdio.h>
2.       #include<conio.h>
3.       #include<alloc.h>
4.       struct node
5.       {
6.               int info;
7.               struct node * link;
8.       };
9.       struct node * getnode();
10.      void addfirst(struct node **, int);
11.      void append(struct node**, int);
12.      void addafter(struct node**, int,int);
13.      void insert_in_sortedlist(struct node **, int);
14.      void delnode(struct node**, int);
15.      void traverse(struct node *);
16.      int count(struct node *);
17.      void freeall(struct node**);
18.      void search(struct node*,int, struct node**,struct node**);
19.      void sort(struct node*);
20.      void reverse(struct node**);
21.      void find(struct node * , int, struct node **);
22.      void main()
23.      {
24.              struct node *p;
25.              int item,pos,cnt,ch;
26.              p = getnode();
27.              p->link = NULL;
28.              do
29.              {
30.                      clrscr();
31.                      printf("1. Addfirst\n2. Append\n3. Addafter\n4. delete\n\
32.              5. Traverse\n6. Count\n7. sort\n8. reverse\n9. Insert\n\
33.                      10. exit\n");
34.                      printf("enter your choice");
35.                      scanf("%d",&ch);
36.                      switch(ch)
37.                      {
38.                              case 1:
39.                                      printf("Enter a number");
40.                                      scanf("%d",&item);
41.                                      addfirst(&p,item);
42.                                      break;
43.                              case 2:
44.                                      printf("Enter a number");
```

```
45.                                    scanf("%d",&item);
46.                                    append(&p,item);
47.                                    break;
48.                    case 3:
49.                                    printf("Enter a number and pos");
50.                                    scanf("%d%d",&item,&pos);
51.                                    addafter(&p,item,pos);
52.                                    break;
53.                    case 4:
54.                                    printf("Enter item to delete");
55.                                    scanf("%d",&item);
56.                                    delnode(&p,item);
57.                                    break;
58.                    case 5:
59.                                    traverse(p);
60.                                    break;
61.                    case 6:
62.                                    cnt = count(p);
63.                                    printf("%d",cnt);
64.                                    break;
65.                    case 7:
66.                                    sort(p);
67.                                    break;
68.                    case 8:
69.                                    reverse(&p);
70.                                    break;
71.                    case 9:
72.                                    printf("Enter item to insert");
73.                                    scanf("%d",&item);
74.                                    insert_in_sortedlist(&p,item);
75.                                    break;
76.                    case 10:
77.                                    freeall(&p);
78.                                    break;
79.                    default:
80.                                    printf("Invalid choice");
81.                    }
82.            getch();
83.        }while(ch != 10);
84.    }
85.    struct node * getnode()
86.    {
87.            struct node * t;
88.            t = (struct node *)malloc(sizeof(struct node));
89.            return (t);
90.    }
```

```
91.     void addfirst(struct node** start, int item)
92.     {
93.             struct node *new;
94.             new = getnode();
95.             if(new == NULL)
96.             {
97.                     printf("Overflow");
98.                     return;
99.             }
100.            new->info = item;
101.            if((*start)->link == NULL)
102.            {
103.                    (*start)->link = new;
104.                    new->link = *start;
105.            }
106.            else
107.            {
108.                    new->link = (*start)->link;
109.                    (*start)->link = new;
110.            }
111.    }
112.    void append(struct node ** start, int item)
113.    {
114.            struct node* new,*ptr;
115.            new = getnode();
116.            if(new == NULL)
117.            {
118.                    printf("Overflow");
119.                    return;
120.            }
121.            new->info = item;
122.            if((*start)->link == NULL)
123.                    (*start)->link = new;
124.            else
125.            {
126.                    ptr = (*start)->link;
127.                    while(ptr->link != *start)
128.                    ptr = ptr->link;
129.                    ptr->link = new;
130.            }
131.            new->link = *start;
132.    }
133.    void traverse(struct node *start)
134.    {
135.            struct node *ptr;
136.            ptr = start->link;
```

```
137.              while(ptr != start)
138.              {
139.                      printf("%d\t",ptr->info);
140.                      ptr = ptr->link;
141.              }
142.      }
143.      int count(struct node *start)
144.      {
145.      struct node *ptr;
146.              int cnt = 0;
147.              ptr = start->link;
148.              while(ptr != start)
149.              {
150.                      cnt++;
151.                      ptr = ptr->link;
152.              }
153.              return (cnt);
154.      }
155.      void freeall(struct node **start)
156.      {
157.              struct node *ptr;
158.              while((*start)->link != NULL)
159.              {
160.                      ptr = (*start)->link;
161.                      *start = (*start)->link;
162.                      free(ptr);
163.              }
164.      }
165.      void search(struct node* start, int item, struct node** loc, struct node** locp)
166.      {
167.              struct node *save,*ptr;
168.              if(start->link == NULL)
169.              {
170.                      *loc = *locp = NULL;
171.                      return;
172.              }
173.              if(item == start->link->info)
174.              {
175.                      *loc = start->link;
176.                      *locp = NULL;
177.                      return;
178.              }
179.              save = start->link;
180.              ptr = start->link->link;
181.              while(ptr != start)
182.              {
```

```
183.                    if(ptr->info == item)
184.                    {
185.                    *loc = ptr;
186.                    *locp = save;
187.              return;
188.                    }
189.                    save = ptr;
190.                    ptr=ptr->link;
191.            }
192.            *loc = *locp = NULL;
193.    }
194.    /* or
195.    void search(struct node* start, int item, struct node** loc, struct node** locp)
196.    {
197.            *locp = NULL;
198.            *loc = start->link;
199.            while(*loc != start && (*loc)->info != item)
200.            {
201.                    *locp = *loc;
202.                    *loc = (*loc)->link;
203.            }
204.    }
205.    */
206.    void delnode(struct node** start, int item)
207.    {
208.            struct node *loc,*locp;
209.            search(*start,item,&loc,&locp);
210.            if(loc == NULL)
211.                    printf("Item not in the list");
212.            else if(locp == NULL)
213.                    (*start)->link = (*start)->link->link;
214.            else
215.                    locp->link = loc->link;
216.            free(loc);
217.    }
218.    void sort(struct node* start)
219.    {
220.            struct node *p1,*p2;
221.            int t;
222.            for(p1=start->link;p1->link != start;p1 = p1->link)
223.                    for(p2= p1->link; p2 != start; p2= p2->link)
224.                            if(p1->info > p2->info)
225.                            {
226.                                    t = p1->info;
227.                                    p1->info = p2->info;
229.                                    p2->info = t;
```

```
230.                                    }
231.    }
232.    void reverse(struct node ** start)
233.    {
234.
235.            struct node *p1,*p2,*p3;
236.            p3 = (*start)->link;
237.            p2 = *start;
238.            while(p3!=*start)
239.            {
240.                    p1 = p2;
241.                    p2 = p3;
242.                    p3=p3->link;
243.                    p2->link = p1;
244.            }
245.            (*start)->link = p2;
246.    }
247.    void addafter(struct node** start, int item, int pos)
248.    {
249.            struct node* new,*ptr;
250.            int i;
251.            for(ptr = (*start)->link, i = 1; i<pos; i++,ptr = ptr->link)
252.            {
253.                    if(ptr == *start)
254.                    {
256.                            printf("Such a node does not exist");
257.                            return;
258.                    }
259.            }
260.            new = getnode();
261.            if(new == NULL)
262.            {
263.                    printf("Overflow");
264.                    return;
265.            }
266.            new->info = item;
267.            new->link = ptr->link;
268.            ptr->link = new;
269.    }
270.    void find(struct node * start, int item, struct node ** loc)
271.    {
272.            struct node *save, *ptr;
273.    if(start->link == NULL || item < start->link->info)
274.            {
275.                    *loc = NULL;
276.                    return;
```

```
277.                  }
278.                  save = start->link;
279.                  ptr = start->link->link;
280.                  while(ptr !=start)
281.                  {
282.                          if(item < ptr->info)
283.                          {
284.                                  *loc = save;
285.                                  return;
286.                          }
287.                          save = ptr;
288.                          ptr = ptr->link;
289.                  }
290.                  *loc = save;
291.          }
292.     void insert_in_sortedlist(struct node **start, int item)
293.     {
294.                  struct node *new,*ptr,*loc;
295.                  find(*start,item,&loc);
296.                  new = getnode();
297.                  if(new == NULL)
298.                  {
299.                          printf("Overflow");
300.                          return ;
301.                  }
302.                  new->info = item;
303.                  if(loc == NULL)
304.                  {
305.                          new->link = (*start)->link;
306.                          (*start)->link = new;
307.                  }
308.                  else
309.                  {
310.                          new->link = loc->link;
311.                          loc->link = new;
312.                  }
313.     }
```

/*Merge two sorted linklist*/

```
1.      #include<stdio.h>
2.      #include<conio.h>
3.      #include<alloc.h>
4.      struct node
5.      {
6.              int info;
```

```
7.                  struct node *link;
8.          };
9.          void append(struct node **,int);
10.         struct node * getnode();
11.         void merge(struct node *, struct node *, struct node **);
12.         void traverse(struct node *);
13.         void main()
14.                 {
15.                 int n1, n2, i,item;
16.                 struct node *l1,*l2,*l3;
17.                 clrscr();
18.                 l1 = l2 = l3 = NULL;
19.                 printf("Enter no. of nodes in first list ");
20.                 scanf("%d",&n1);
21.                 for(i=0;i<n1;i++)
22.                     {
23.                         printf("Enter item to append in the list ");
24.                         scanf("%d",&item);
25.                         append(&l1,item);
26.                     }
27.         printf("Enter no. of nodes in first second list ");
28.                 scanf("%d",&n2);
29.                 for(i=0;i<n2;i++)
30.                     {
31.                         printf("Enter item to append in the second list ");
32.                         scanf("%d",&item);
33.                         append(&l2,item);
34.                     }
35.                 printf("\nFirst List is \n");
36.                 traverse(l1);
37.                 printf("\nSecond list is\n");
38.                 traverse(l2);
39.                 merge(l1,l2,&l3);
40.                 printf("\nThird list is\n");
41.                 traverse(l3);
42.                 getch();
43.         }
44.         void append(struct node ** start, int item)
45.         {
46.                 struct node* new,*ptr;
47.                 new = getnode();
48.                 if(new == NULL)
49.                     {
50.                         printf("Overflow");
51.                         return;
52.                     }
```

```
53.              new->info = item;
54.              new->link = NULL;
55.              if(*start == NULL)
56.                      *start = new;
57.              else
58.              {
59.                      ptr = *start;
60.                      while(ptr->link != NULL)
61.                              ptr = ptr->link;
62.                      ptr->link = new;
63.              }
64.      }
65.      struct node * getnode()
67.      {
68.              struct node * t;
69.              t = (struct node *)malloc(sizeof(struct node));
70.              return (t);
71.      }
72.      void traverse(struct node *start)
73.      {
74.              struct node *ptr;
75.              ptr = start;
76.              while(ptr != NULL)
77.              {
78.                      printf("%d\t",ptr->info);
79.                      ptr = ptr->link;
80.              }
81.      }
82.      void merge(struct node *l1, struct node *l2, struct node **l3)
83.      {
84.              while(l1 !=NULL && l2 != NULL)
85.              {
86.                      if(l1->info < l2->info)
87.                      {
88.                              append(l3,l1->info);
89.                              l1 = l1->link;
90.                      }
91.                      else
92.                      {
93.                              append(l3,l2->info);
94.                              l2 = l2->link;
95.                      }
96.              }
97.      /*remaining of 1st list*/
98.              while(l1!= NULL)
99.              {
```

```
100.                        append(l3,l1->info);
101.                        l1 = l1->link;
102.             }
103.             /*remaining of 1st list*/
104.             while(l2!= NULL)
105.             {
106.                        append(l3,l2->info);
107.                        l2 = l2->link;
108.             }
109.    }
```

/*Add two polynomial equations using linklist*/

```
1.      #include<stdio.h>
2.      #include<conio.h>
3.      #include<alloc.h>
4.      #include<math.h>
5.      struct node
6.              {
7.              int coeff,pow;
8.              struct node *link;
                };
9.      void append(struct node **,int,int);
10.     struct node * getnode();
11.     void add_poly(struct node *, struct node *, struct node **);
12.     void traverse(struct node *);
13.     void main()
14.     {
15.             int n1, n2, i,c,p;
16.             struct node *l1,*l2,*l3;
17.             clrscr();
18.             l1 = l2 = l3 = NULL;
19.             printf("Enter no. of terms in first equation ");
20.             scanf("%d",&n1);
21.             for(i=0;i<n1;i++)
22.             {
23.                     printf("Enter coeff and power of x ");
24.                     scanf("%d%d",&c,&p);
25.                     append(&l1,c,p);
26.             }
27.             printf("Enter no. of nodes in second equation ");
28.             scanf("%d",&n2);
29.             for(i=0;i<n2;i++)
30.             {
31.                     printf("Enter coeff and power of x ");
32.                     scanf("%d%d",&c,&p);
```

```
33.                       append(&l2,c,p);
34.               }
35.               printf("\nFirst eqation is \n");
36.               traverse(l1);
37.               printf("\nSecond equation is\n");
38.               traverse(l2);
39.               add_poly(l1,l2,&l3);
40.               printf("\nThird equation is\n");
41.               traverse(l3);
42.               getch();
43.       }
44.       void append(struct node ** start, int c, int p)
45.       {
46.               struct node* new,*ptr;
47.               new = getnode();
48.               if(new == NULL)
49.               {
50.                       printf("Overflow");
51.                       return;
52.               }
53.               new->coeff = c;
54.               new->pow = p;
55.               new->link = NULL;
56.               if(*start == NULL)
57.                       *start = new;
58.               else
59.               {
60.                       ptr = *start;
61.                       while(ptr->link != NULL)
62.                               ptr = ptr->link;
63.                       ptr->link = new;
64.               }
65.       }
66.       struct node * getnode()
67.       {
68.               struct node * t;
69.               t = (struct node *)malloc(sizeof(struct node));
70.               return (t);
71.       }
72.       void traverse(struct node *start)
73.       {
74.               struct node *ptr;
75.               ptr = start;
76.               while(ptr != NULL)
77.               {
78.                       if(ptr->coeff > 0)
```

```c
79.                     printf("+ %dx^%d ",ptr->coeff,ptr->pow);
80.                     else
81.                     printf("- %dx^%d ",abs(ptr->coeff),ptr->pow);
82.                     ptr = ptr->link;
83.             }
84.     }
85.     void add_poly(struct node *l1, struct node *l2, struct node **l3)
86.     {
87.             while(l1 !=NULL && l2 != NULL)
89.             {
90.                     if(l1->pow == l2->pow)
91.                     {
92.                             append(l3,l1->coeff+l2->coeff,l1->pow);
93.                             l1 = l1->link;
94.                             l2 = l2->link;
95.                     }
96.                     else if(l1->pow > l2->pow)
97.                     {
98.                             append(l3,l1->coeff,l1->pow);
99.                             l1 = l1->link;
100.                    }
101.                    else
102.                    {
103.                            append(l3,l2->coeff,l2->pow);
104.                            l2 = l2->link;
105.                    }
106.            }
107.            /*remaining of 1st list*/
108.            while(l1!= NULL)
109.            {
110.                    append(l3,l1->coeff,l1->pow);
111.                    l1 = l1->link;
112.            }
113.            /*remaining of 1st list*/
114.            while(l2!= NULL)
115.            {
116.                    append(l3,l2->coeff,l2->pow);
117.                    l2 = l2->link;
118.            }
119.    }
```

/*Multiply two Polynomial equations*/

```c
1.      #include<stdio.h>
2.      #include<conio.h>
3.      struct node
4.      {
5.              int coeff,pow;
6.              struct node *link;
7.      };
8.      void insert(struct node **, int, int);
9.      void traverse(struct node *);
10.     struct node *getnode();
11.     struct node * mult_list(struct node *, struct node *);
12.     void main()
13.     {
14.             int c,p,n,i;
15.             struct node *l1,*l2,*l3;
16.             clrscr();
17.             l1 = l2 = l3 = NULL;
18.             printf("Enter no. of terms in first equation");
19.             scanf("%d",&n);
20.             for(i=0;i<n;i++)
21.             {
22.                     printf("Enter coeff and power");
23.                     scanf("%d %d",&c, &p);
24.                     insert(&l1,c,p);
25.             }
26.             printf("\nEnter no. of terms in second equation");
27.             scanf("%d",&n);
28.             for(i=0;i<n;i++)
29.             {
30.                     printf("Enter coeff and power");
31.                     scanf("%d %d",&c, &p);
32.                     insert(&l2,c,p);
33.             }
34.             printf("\nFirst equation is \n");
35.             traverse(l1);
36.             printf("\nSecond equation is \n");
37.             traverse(l2);
38.             l3 = mult_list(l1,l2);
39.             printf("\nMultiply list is \n");
40.             traverse(l3);
41.             getch();
42.     }
43.     struct node * getnode()
44.     {
```

```
45.              struct node *t;
46.              t = (struct node *)malloc(sizeof(struct node));
47.              return (t);
48.      }
49.      void traverse(struct node *p)
50.      {
51.              while(p!=NULL)
52.              {
53.                      if(p->coeff >= 0)
54.                              printf("+%dx%d",p->coeff,p->pow);
55.                      else
56.                              printf("%dx%d ",p->coeff,p->pow);
57.                      p=p->link;
58.              }
59.      }
60.      void insert(struct node** p,int c, int pow)
61.      {
62.              struct node *t,*q;
63.                      q = *p;
64.              if(q == NULL)
65.              {
66.                      t = getnode();
67.                      t->coeff = c;
68.                      t->pow = pow;
69.                      t->link = NULL;
70.                      *p = t;
71.              }
72.              else
73.              {
74.                      while(q->link != NULL && q->pow != pow)
75.                              q = q->link;
76.                      if(q->pow==pow)
77.                              q->coeff = q->coeff + c;
78.                      else
79.                      {
80.                              t = getnode();
81.                              t->coeff = c;
82.                              t->pow = pow;
83.                              t->link = q->link;
84.                              q->link = t;
85.                      }
86.              }
87.      }
88.      struct node * mult_list(struct node *l1, struct node *l2)
89.      {
90.              struct node *p1,*p2,*p3;
```

```c
91.              int coeff,pow;
92.              if(l1 == NULL)
93.                      return l2;
94.              if(l2 == NULL)
95.                      return l1;
96.              p3 = NULL;
97.              p1 = l1;
98.         while(p1!=NULL)
99.              {
100.                     p2 = l2;
101.                     while(p2!=NULL)
102.                     {
103.                             coeff = p1->coeff * p2->coeff;
104.                             pow = p1->pow + p2->pow;
105.                             insert(&p3,coeff,pow);
106.                             p2 = p2->link;
107.                     }
108.                     p1=p1->link;
109.             }
110.             return (p3);
111.    }
```

/* Stack using linklist */

```c
1.       #include<stdio.h>
2.       #include<conio.h>
3.       struct node
4.       {
5.               int info;
6.               struct node*link;
7.       };
8.
9.       void push(struct node **,int );
10.      int pop(struct node **);
11.      int peep(struct node*);
12.      struct node * getnode();
13.      void main()
14.      {
15.              int ch,item;
16.              struct node *p;
17.              p = NULL;
18.              do
19.              {
20.                      clrscr();
21.                      printf("\t\t\tMAIN MENU\n");
22.                      printf("\t\t\t********\n\n");
```

```
23.                    printf("\t\t 1. Push in a Stack.\n");
24.                    printf("\t\t 2. Pop from the Stack.\n");
25.                    printf("\t\t 3. Stack Top or Peep.\n");
26.                    printf("\t\t 4. Exit.\n\n");
27.                    printf("\t\t Enter your choice:- ");
28.                    scanf("%d",&ch);
29.                    clrscr();
30.                    switch(ch)
31.                    {
32.                          case 1:
33.                    printf("Enter the value which is to be Push:- ");
34.                                scanf("%d",&item);
35.                                push(&p,item);
36.                                break;
37.                          case 2:
38.                                item=pop(&p);
39.                                if(item != NULL)
40.                    printf("Pop Value==> %d",item);
41.                                break;
42.                          case 3:
43.                                item=peep(p);
44.                                if(item != NULL)
45.                    printf("Stack Top Value==> %d",item);
46.                                break;
47.                          case 4:
48.                                break;
49.                          default:
50.                    printf("Wrong Choice !.Try Again .");
51.                    }
52.                    getch();
53.             }while(ch != 4);
54.      }
55.      void push(struct node **top,int item)
56.      {
57.             struct node *new;
58.             new = getnode();
59.             if(new == NULL)
60.             {
61.                    printf("Overflow");
62.                    return;
63.             }
64.             new->info = item;
65.             new->link = *top;
66.             *top = new;
67.      }
68.      int pop(struct node **top)
```

```
68.     {
69.             struct node *ptr;
70.             int item;
71.             if(*top == NULL)
72.             {
73.                     printf("Underflow");
74.                     return (NULL);
75.             }
76.             ptr = *top;
77.             *top = (*top)->link;
78.             item = ptr->info;
79.             free(ptr);
80.             return(item);
81.     }
82.     int peep(struct node *top)
83.     {
85.             int item;
86.             if(top == NULL)
87.             {
88.                     printf("Underflow");
89.                     return (NULL);
90.             }
91.             item = top->info;
92.             return(item);
93.     }
94.     struct node * getnode()
95.     {
96.             struct node * t;
97.             t = (struct node *)malloc(sizeof(struct node));
98.             return (t);
99.     }
```

/* Queue using linklist */

```
1.      #include<stdio.h>
2.      #include<conio.h>
3.      struct node
4.      {
5.              int info;
6.              struct node *link;
7.      };
8.      void addq(struct node **,struct node **,int );
9.      int delq(struct node **,struct node **);
10.     struct node * getnode();
11.     void main()
12.     {
```

```
13.                int ch,item;
14.                struct node *p,*q;
15.                p = q = NULL;
16.                do
17.                {
18.                        clrscr();
19.                        printf("\t\t\tMAIN MENU\n");
20.                        printf("\t\t\t********\n\n");
21.                        printf("\t\t 1. Add in a Queue.\n");
22.                        printf("\t\t 2. Delete from the Queue.\n");
23.                        printf("\t\t 3. Exit.\n\n");
24.                        printf("\t\t Enter your choice:- ");
25.                        scanf("%d",&ch);
26.                        clrscr();
27.                        switch(ch)
28.                        {
29.                                case 1:
30.                                        printf("Enter the value :- ");
31.                                        scanf("%d",&item);
32.                                        addq(&p,&q,item);
33.                                        break;
34.                                case 2:
35.                                        item=delq(&p,&q);
36.                                        if(item != NULL)
37.                                printf("Deleted Value==> %d",item);
38.                                        break;
39.                                case 3:
40.                                        break;
41.                                default:
42.                                        printf("Wrong Choice !.Try Again
.");
43.                        }
44.                        getch();
45.                }while(ch != 3);
46.        }
47.     void addq(struct node **front, struct node **rear,int item)
48.     {
49.                struct node *new;
50.                new = getnode();
51.                if(new == NULL)
52.                {
53.                        printf("Overflow");
54.                        return;
55.                }
56.                new->info = item;
57.                new->link = NULL;
```

```
58.            if(*front == NULL)
59.                    *front = *rear = new;
60.            else
61.            {
62.                    (*rear)->link = new;
63.                    *rear = new;
64.            }
65.    }
66.    int delq(struct node **front, struct node **rear)
67.    {
68.            struct node *ptr;
69.            int item;
70.            if(*front == NULL)
71.            {
72.                    printf("Underflow");
73.                    return (NULL);
74.            }
75.            ptr = *front;
76.            if(*front == *rear)
77.                    *front = *rear = NULL;
78.            else
79.                    *front = (*front)->link;
80.            item = ptr->info;
81.            free(ptr);
82.            return(item);
83.    }
84.    struct node * getnode()
85.    {
86.            struct node * t;
87.            t = (struct node *)malloc(sizeof(struct node));
88.            return (t);
89.    }
```

Doubly Linked List

CHAPTER
∞ **8** ∞
(TREE IN DSA)

Introduction-

Tree is a nonlinear data structure. This structure is mainly used to represent data containing a hierarchical relationship between elements, e.g., records, family trees and tables of contents.

❖ **Type of trees:**

Binary Tree:

A Binary tree is either empty, or it consists of a node called the root together with two binary trees called the left sub-tree and the right sub-tree of the root.

Total number of binary trees with N nodes = $\frac{2N C N}{(N+1)}$ = 2n! / (n! (n+1)!)

- ❖ BST-Binary Search Tree.
- ❖ AVL Tree.
- ❖ Heap Tree.
- ❖ 2 Tree or Extended Binary Tree.
- ❖ Huffman Tree.
- ❖ Threaded Binary Tree.

General Tree:

- ❖ MST-Multi-way Search Tree.
- ❖ B Tree.
- ❖ B+ Tree.

BST (Binary Search Tree):
A binary Search Tree is a binary tree that is either empty or in which each node contains a key that satisfies the conditions:

1.All keys (if any) in the left sub-tree of the root precede the key in the root.

2.The key in the root precedes all keys (if any) in its right sub-tree.

3. The left and right sub-trees of the root are again search trees.

AVL Tree:
An AVL tree is a binary search tree in which the heights of the left and right sub-trees of the root differ by at most 1 and in which the left and right sub-trees are again AVL trees.

With each node of an AVL tree is associated a balance factor that is left high, equal, or right high according, respectively, as the left sub-tree has height greater than, equal to, or less than that of the right sub-tree.

HEAP Tree:

A heap is defined to be a binary tree with a key in each node, such that.

1. All the leaves of the tree are on two adjacent levels.

2. All leaves on the lowest level occur to the left and all levels, except possibly the lowest, are filled.

3. The key in the root is at least as large as the keys in its children (if any), and the left and right sub-trees (if they exist) are again heaps.

2 Tree:

A binary tree T is said to be a 2-tree or an extended binary tree if each node N has either 0 or 2 children. In such a case, the nodes with 2 children are called internal nodes,

And the nodes with 0 children are called external nodes. Sometimes the nodes are distinguished in diagrams by using circles for internal nodes and squares for external nodes.

Threaded Binary Tree:

In a binary tree approximately half of the entries in the pointer fields LEFT and RIGHT will contain null elements.

This space may be more efficiently used by replacing the null entries by some other type of information. Specifically, we will replace certain null entries by special pointers which point to nodes higher in the tree.

These special pointers are called threads, and binary trees with such pointers are called threaded trees.

The threads in a threaded tree must be distinguish threads from ordinary pointers. The threads in a diagram of a threaded tree are usually indicated by dotted lines. In computer memory, an extra 1-bit TAG field may be used to distinguish threads from ordinary pointers, or, alternatively, threads may be denoted by negative integers when ordinary pointers are denoted by positive integers.

There are many ways to thread a binary tree T, but each threading will correspond to a particular traversal of T. Also, one may choose a one-way threading or a two-way threading. Unless otherwise stated, our threading will correspond to the inorder traversal of T.

Threaded binary tree can be traversed without using a stack in pre-order or in-order but post-order is not possible using any threaded binary tree.

MST (Multi-way Search Tree):

A multi-way tree is also called as multi-way search tree or a m-way tree. It is a general search tree where each node may contain one or more keys and there can be more than two children(sub-trees) for each node.

A multi-way search tree of order n is a tree where each node has n or less than n sub-trees and contains one less key than it has sub-trees.

If a node has four sub-tree then it contains three keys If the children of that node are s1, s2, s3, s4 and keys stored in that node are k1, k2, k3 then s1 is the left son of k1 and s2 is the right son of k1.

Because it is a search tree so all the keys in the left sub-tree of k1 must be smaller than k1 and all the keys in the right sub-tree of k1 must be greater than k1. It means k1 partitions the keys in s1 and s2.

Type of multi-way search trees-

1. Normal Multi-way Search tree.
2. Top down multi-way search tree : - If any non-full node is a leaf.
3. Balanced multi-way search tree. :- B-Tree.

Difference Point of difference	BST	MST
1. Max No. of child	In BST there can be maximum two Childs	In MST there can be n child Where n is the order of the tree
2. Max no. of keys	In BST there can be maximum one key in each node	In MST there can be maximum n-1 keys. Where n is the order of the tree each node
3. Height	In BST the height is more	In MST height of the tree is less
4. Scope	BST can be well suited for internal searching access.	MST can be used in external searching to reduce the number of disk
5. Balance	AVL tree is the Balanced BST	B tree is the balanced MST.

Resemblence:
1. Both type of tree are designed for searching. So any Key value is greater than all the keys in its left subtree and it is smaller than all the keys in its right subtree.

2. Both trees if traversed in inorder will display the tree in ascending order.

3. Searching time is same in both trees i.e. O(log n)

Insertion in a multiway search tree (Top down search tree):

We assume that duplicate key is not allowed in the multiway tree, so that if the key is found in the tree no insertion takes place. We also assume that the tree is non-empty.

The first step is to search for the key. If the key is found in the tree, we return a pointer to the node containing the key and set the variable position to its position within the node.

However if the key is not found we return a pointer to the semileaf node(s) that would contain the key if it were present and position is set to the index of the smallest key in node(s) that is greater than the key. If all the keys in node are less than the key position is set to maxchild i.e. order of the tree.

B-Tree:
A B-tree of order n is a balanced multi-way search tree in which.

1. All leaves are on the same level.

2. All internal nodes except the root have at most n (non-empty) children, and at least [n/2] (nonempty) children.

3. The number of keys in each internal node is one less than the number of its children,, and these keys partition the keys in the children in the fachion of a search tree.

4. The root has at most n children, but may have as few as 2 if it is not a leaf, or none if the tree consists of the root alone.

5. All nodes can contain at most N-1 keys and at least (N-1)/2 keys.

Algorithm

FIND (INFO, LEFT, RIGHT, ROOT, ITEM, LOC, PAR)

A binary search tree T is in memory and an ITEM of information is given. This procedure finds the location LOC of ITEM in T and the location PAR of the parent of ITEM. There are three special cases:

1. LOC = NULL and PAR = NULL will indicate that the tree is empty.

2. LOC ≠ NULL and PAR = NULL will indicate that ITEM is the root of T.

3. LOC = NULL and PAR ≠ NULL will indicate that ITEM is not in T and can be added to T as a child of the node N with location PAR.

1.   [Tree empty?]
        If ROOT = NULL, then: Set LOC: = NULL and PAR: = NULL, and Return.
2.   [ITEM at root?]
        If ITEM = INFO [ROOT], then: Set LOC: = ROOT and PAR: = NULL, and Return.
3.   [Initialize pointers PTR and SAVE.]
        If ITEM < INFO [ROOT], then:
                        Set PTR: = LEFT [ROOT] and SAVE: = ROOT.

Else:
                    Set PTR: = RIGHT [ROOT] and SAVE: = ROOT.
            [End of If structure.]
4.   Repeat Steps 5 and 6 while PTR ≠ NULL:
5.   [ITEM found?]
                If ITEM = INFO [PTR], then: Set LOC: = PTR and PAR: = SAVE,
                    and Return.
6.   If ITEM < INFO [PTR], then:
                            Set SAVE: = PTR and PTR: = LEFT [PTR].
                Else:
                            Set SAVE: = PTR and PTR: = RIGHT [PTR].
                [End of If structure.]
            [End of step 4 loop.]
7.   [Search unsuccessful.] Set LOC: = NULL and PAR: = SAVE.
8.   Exit.

INSBST (INFO, LEFT, RIGHT, ROOT, AVAIL, ITEM, LOC)

A binary search tree T is in memory and an ITEM of information is given. This algorithm finds the location LOC of ITEM in T or adds ITEM as a new node in T at location LOC.

1.   Call FIND (INFO, LEFT, RIGHT, ROOT, AVAIL, ITEM, LOC, and PAR).
2.   If LOC ≠ NULL, then Exit.
3.   [Copy ITEM into new node in AVAIL list.]
        (a)   If AVAIL = NULL, then: Write: OVERFLOW, and Exit.
        (b)   Set NEW: = AVAIL, AVAIL: = LEFT [AVAIL] and INFO [NEW]:
                = ITEM.
        (c)   Set LOC: = NEW, LEFT [NEW]: = NULL and RIGHT [NEW]: =
                NULL.
4.   [Add ITEM to tree.]
                If PAR = NULL then;
                        Set ROOT: = NEW.
                Else if ITEM < INFO [PAR], then:
                        Set LEFT [PAR]: = NEW.
                Else:
                            Set RIGHT [PAR]: = NEW.
                [End of If structure.]
5.   Exit.

CASEA (INFO, LEFT, RIGHT, ROOT, LOC, PAR)

This procedure deletes the node N at location LOC, where N does not have two children. The pointer PAR gives the location of the parent of N, or else PAR= NULL indicates that N is the root node.

The pointer CHILD gives the location of the only child of N, or else CHILD = NULL indicates N has no children.

1.   [Initializes CHILD.]
        If LEFT [LOC] = NULL and RIGHT [LOC] = NULL, then:
                Set CHILD: = NULL.
        Else if LEFT [LOC] ≠ NULL then:
                Set CHILD: = LEFT [LOC].
        Else:
                Set CHILD: = RIGHT [LOC].
        [End of If structure.]
2.   If PAR ≠ NULL then:
                If LOC = LEFT [PAR], then:
                        Set LEFT [PAR]: = CHILD.
                Else:
                        Set RIGHT [PAR]: = CHILD.
                [End of if structure.]
        Else:
                Set ROOT: = CHILD.
        [End of If structure.]
3.   Return.

CASEB (INFO, LEFT, RIGHT, ROOT, LOC, PAR)

This procedure deletes the node N at location LOC, where N has two children. The pointer PAR gives the location of the parent of N, or else PAR= NULL indicates that N is the root node. The pointer SUC gives the location of the in-order successor of N, and PARSUC gives the location of the parent of the in-order successor.

1.   [Find SUC and PARSUC.]
        (a) Set PTR: = RIGHT [LOC] and SAVE: = LOC.
        (b) Repeat while LEFT [PTR] ≠ NULL:
                        Set SAVE: = PTR and PTR: = LEFT [PTR].
                [End of loop.]
        (c) Set SUC: = PTR and PARSUC: = SAVE.
2.   [Delete in-order successor, using Procedure CASEA.]

                CASEA (INFO, LEFT, RIGHT, ROOT, SUC, PARSUC)
3.   [Replace node N by its in-order successor.]
                (a)   If PAR ≠ NULL, then:
                                If LOC = LEFT [PTR], then:
                                        Set LEFT [PAR]: = SUC.
                                Else:
                                        Set RIGHT [PAR]: = SUC.

[End of if structure.]
                Else:
                        Set ROOT: = SUC.
                [End of if structure.]
        (b)   Set LEFT [SUC]: = LEFT [LOC] and
                RIGHT [SUC]: = RIGHT [LOC].
4.   Return.

DEL (INFO, LEFT, RIGHT, ROOT, AVAIL, ITEM)

A binary search tree T is in memory and an ITEM of information is given. This algorithm deletes ITEM from the tree.

1.   [Find the locations of ITEM and its parent, using Procedure FIND]
                Call FIND (INFO, LEFT, RIGHT, ROOT, ITEM, LOC, PAR)
2.   [ITEM in tree?]
                If LOC = NULL, then: Write: ITEM not in tree and Exit.
3.   [Deletes node containing ITEM.]
                If RIGHT [LOC] ≠ NULL and LEFT [LOC] ≠ NULL, then:
                        Call CASEB (INFO, LEFT, RIGHT, ROOT, LOC, PAR)
                Else:
                        Call CASEA (INFO, LEFT, RIGHT, ROOT, LOC, PAR)
                [End of If structure.]
4.   [Return deleted node to the AVAIL list.]
                Set LEFT [LOC]: = AVAIL and AVAIL: = LOC.
5.   Exit.

PREORD (INFO, LEFT, RIGHT, ROOT)

A binary tree T is in memory. The algorithm does a preorder traversal of T, applying an operation PROCESS to each of its nodes. An array STACK is used to temporarily hold the address of nodes.
1.   [Initially push NULL onto STACK, and initialize PTR.]
        Set TOP: = 1 , STACK [1]: = NULL and PTR: = ROOT.
2.   Repeat Steps 3 to 5 while PTR ≠ NULL:
3.   Apply PROCESS to INFO [PTR].
4.   [Right child?]
                If RIGHT [PTR] ≠ NULL, then: [Push on STACK.]
                Set TOP: = TOP +1, and STACK [TOP]: = RIGHT [PTR].
                [End of If structure.]
5.   [Left child?]
                If LEFT [PTR] ≠ NULL, then:
                        Set PTR: = LEFT [PTR].
                Else: [Pop from STACK.]
                        Set PTR: = STACK [TOP] and TOP: = TOP-1.

[End of If structure.]
[End of Step 2 loop.]
6.   Exit.

INORD (INFO, LEFT, RIGHT, ROOT)

A binary tree is in memory. This algorithm does an in-order traversal of T, applying an operation PROCESS to each of its nodes. An array STACK is used to temporarily hold the addresses of nodes.

1.   [Push NULL onto STACK and initialize PTR.]
                Set TOP: = 1, STACK [1]: = NULL and PTR: = ROOT.
2.   Repeat while PTR ≠ NULL: [Pushes left-most path onto STACK.]
                (a) Set TOP: = TOP + 1 and STACK [TOP]: = PTR. [Saves node.]
                (b) Set PTR: = LEFT [PTR]. [Updates PTR.]
                [End of loop.]
3.   Set PTR: = STACK [TOP] and TOP: = TOP – 1 [Pops node from STACK.]
4.   Repeat Steps 5 to 7 while PTR ≠ NULL: [Backtracking.]
5.   Apply PROCESS to INFO [PTR].
6.   [Right child?] If RIGHT [PTR] ≠ NULL, then:
                        (a) Set PTR: = RIGHT [PTR].
                        (b) Go to Step 2.
                [End of If structure.]
7.   Set PTR: = STACK [TOP] and TOP: = TOP – 1. [Pops node.]
        [End of Step 4 loop.]
8.   Exit.

POSTORD (INFO, LEFT, RIGHT, ROOT)

A binary tree T is in memory. This algorithm does a post-order traversal of T, applying an operation PROCESS to each of its nodes. An array STACK is used to temporarily hold the addresses of nodes.

1.   [Push NULL onto STACK and initialize PTR.]
                Set TOP: = 1, STACK [1]:= NULL and PTR := ROOT.
2.   [Push left-most path onto STACK.]
                Repeat Steps 3 to 5 while PTR ≠ NULL:
3.   Set TOP: = TOP +1 and STACK [TOP]: =PTR.
                [Pushes PTR on STACK.]
4.   If RIGHT [PTR] ≠ NULL, then: [Push on STACK.,]
                        Set TOP: = TOP + 1 and STACK [TOP]: = -RIGHT [PTR].
                RIGHT [PTR].
                [End of If structure.]
5.   Set PTR: = LEFT [PTR]. [Updates pointer PTR.]

[End of Step 2 loop.]
6.   Set PTR: = STACK [TOP] and TOP: = TOP – 1
                [Pops node from STACK.]
7.   Repeat while PTR > 0:
                (a) Apply PROCESS to INFO [PTR].
                (b) Set PTR: = STACK [TOP] and [TOP]: = TOP –1.
            [Pops node from STACK.]
            [End of loop.]
8.   If PTR< 0, then:
                (a) Set PTR: = -PTR.
                (b) Go to Step 2.
                [End of If structure.]
9.   Exit.

PREORD (INFO, LEFT, RIGHT, ROOT)

        This is a recursive procedure to traverse the tree starting from root in preorder (i.e.   root, left , right) and APPLY a PROCESS of INFO of each node...

1.   If ROOT = NULL, then: Return.
2.   Apply a PROCESS on INFO [ROOT].
3.   Call PREORD (INFO, LEFT, RIGHT, LEFT [ROOT]).
4.   Call PREORD (INFO, LEFT, RIGHT, RIGHT [ROOT]).
5.   Return.

INORD (INFO, LEFT, RIGHT, ROOT)

        This is a recursive procedure to traverse the tree starting from root in in-order (i.e.   left, root, right) and APPLY a PROCESS of INFO of each node.

1.   If ROOT = NULL, then: Return.
2.   Call INORD (INFO, LEFT, RIGHT, LEFT [ROOT]).
3.   Apply a PROCESS on INFO [ROOT].
4.   Call INORD (INFO, LEFT, RIGHT, RIGHT [ROOT]).
5.   Return.

POSTORD (INFO, LEFT, RIGHT, ROOT)

This is a recursive procedure to traverse the tree starting from root in post-order (i.e.   left, right, root) and APPLY a PROCESS of INFO of each node.

1   If ROOT = NULL, then: Return.
2.   Call POSTORD (INFO, LEFT, RIGHT, LEFT [ROOT]).
3.   Call POSTORD (INFO, LEFT, RIGHT, RIGHT [ROOT]).
4.   Apply a PROCESS on INFO [ROOT].
5.   Return.

COUNT (LEFT, RIGHT, ROOT, NUM)

This procedure finds the number NUM of nodes in a binary tree T in memory.

1.   If ROOT = NULL, then: Set NUM: = 0 , and Return.
2.   Call COUNT (LEFT, RIGHT, LEFT [ROOT], NUML).
3.   Call COUNT (LEFT, RIGHT, RIGHT [ROOT], NUMR).
4.   Set NUM: = NUML + NUMR + 1.
5.   Return.

DEPTH (LEFT, RIGHT, ROOT, DEP)

This procedure finds the depth DEP of a binary tree T in memory.

1.   If ROOT = NULL, then: Set DEP: = 0, and Return.
2.   Call DEPTH (LEFT, RIGHT, LEFT [ROOT], DEPL).
3.   Call DEPTH (LEFT, RIGHT, RIGHT [ROOT], DEPR).
4.   If DEPL >= DEPR, then:
                Set DEP: = DEPL + 1.
        Else:
                Set DEP: = DEPR + 1.
        [End of If structure.]
5.   Return.

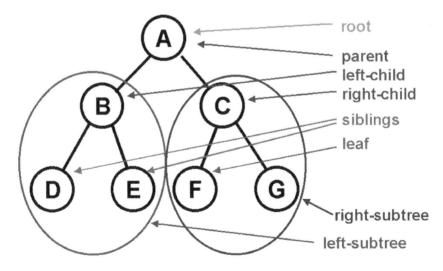

C Programs

BST (Binary Search Tree)
/* **Insert in BST, Deletion in BST, Traverse Recursive pre, post, in traverse nonrecursive pre,in, counting nodes, counting depth, searching**/

```
1.      #include<stdio.h>
2.      #include<conio.h>
3.      #include<alloc.h>
4.      #define MAXSTK 50
5.      struct node
6.      {
7.              struct node *left;
8.              struct node *right;
9.              int info;
10.     };
11.     struct stack /* For Non-Recursive Traverse of BST*/
12.     {
13.             int top;
14.             struct node * info[MAXSTK];
15.     };
16.     struct node * getnode();
17.     void insert(struct node ** ,int );
18.     void search(struct node * , int , struct node ** , struct node ** );
19.     void delnode(struct node ** ,int );
20.     void casea(struct node ** ,struct node **, struct node ** );
21.     void caseb(struct node ** , struct node **, struct node** );
22.     int count(struct node * );
23.     int depth(struct node *);
24.     /*Recursive*/
25.     void traverse(struct node * );
26.     void pre_trav(struct node * );
27.     void post_trav(struct node * );
28.     void in_trav(struct node * );
29.     /*Non Recursive*/
30.     void traverse2(struct node * );
31.     void pre_trav2(struct node *);
32.     void post_trav2(struct node * );
33.     void in_trav2(struct node * );
34.     void push(struct stack *,struct node *);
35.     struct node * pop(struct stack *);
36.     /* Main Function Starts*/
37.     void main()
38.     {
39.             int item, ch;
```

```c
40.                 struct node *p = NULL,*par,*loc;
41.                 clrscr();
42.                 do
43.                 {
44.                         clrscr();
45.                         printf("\t\t\tMAIN MENU\n");
46.                         printf("\t\t\t********\n\n");
47.                         printf("\t\t 1.Insertion in the Tree.\n");
48.                         printf("\t\t 2.Deletion from the Tree.\n");
49.                         printf("\t\t 3.Traverse of Tree(Recursive).\n");
50.                         printf("\t\t 4.Traverse of Tree(Non Recursive).\n");
51.                         printf("\t\t 5.Counting of Nodes in Tree.\n");
52.                         printf("\t\t 6.Counting depth in Tree.\n");
53.                         printf("\t\t 7.Searching of Node in Tree.\n");
54.                         printf("\t\t 8.Exit.\n\n");
55.                         printf("\t\t Enter your choice:- ");
56.                         scanf("%d",&ch);
57.                         clrscr();
58.                         switch(ch)
59.                         {
60.                         case 1:
61.                                 printf("Enter value to Insert in the tree:- ");
62.                                 scanf("%d",&item);
63.                                 clrscr();
64.                                 /* Calling of Insert Function */
66.                                 insert(&p,item);
67.                                 break;
68.                         case 2:
69.                                 printf("Enter Value to delete:- ");
70.                                 scanf("%d",&item);
71.                                 clrscr();
72.                                 /* Calling of Delete Function */
73.                                 delnode(&p,item);
74.                                 break;
76.                         case 3:
77.                                 /* Calling of Traverse Function */
78.                                 traverse(p);
79.                                 break;
80.                         case 4:
81.                                 /* Calling of Traverse Function */
82.                                 traverse2(p);
83.                                 break;
84.                         case 5:
85.                                 /* Calling of Count Function */
86.                                 printf("%d",count(p));
87.                                 break;
```

```
88.                         case 6:
89.                                 /* Calling of Count Function */
90.                                 printf("%d",depth(p));
91.                                 break;
92.                 case 7:
93.                         printf("Enter a Value Which is to be searched:- ");
94.                                 scanf("%d",&item);
95.                                 clrscr();
96.                                 /* Calling of Search Function */
97.                                 search(p,item,&par,&loc);
98.                                 if(loc != NULL)
99.                         printf("Given Node Exist in the Tree.");
100.                                else
101.                        printf("Given Node Does Not Exist.");
102.                                break;
103.                        case 8:
104.                                break;
105.                        default:
106.                        printf("Wrong Choice !. Try Again. ");
107.                        }
108.                getch();
109.        }while(ch!=8);
110.    }
111.    struct node *getnode()
112.    {
113.            struct node *t;
114.            t = (struct node *)malloc(sizeof(struct node));
115.            t->right = NULL;
116.            t->left = NULL;
117.            return(t);
118.    }
119.    void insert(struct node **root,int item)
120.    {
121.            struct node *par,*loc,ptr,*new;
122.            /* Calling of Search Function */
123.            search(*root,item,&par,&loc);
124.            if(loc != NULL)
125.            {
126.                    printf("Duplicate Value.Therefore,We can't insert.");
127.                    return;
128.            }
129.            new = getnode();
130.            new->info = item;
131.            if(par == NULL)
132.            {
133.                    *root = new;
```

```
134.                        return;
135.              }
136.              else if(item > par->info )
137.                          par->right = new;
138.              else
139.                          par->left = new;
140.      }
141.      void search(struct node *root,int item,struct node **par,struct node **loc)
142.      {
143              struct node *ptr,*save;
144.              if(root == NULL)
145.              {
146.                          *loc = NULL;
147.                          *par = NULL;
148.                          return;
149.              }
150.              if(item == root->info)
151.              {
152.                          *loc = root;
153.                          *par = NULL;
154.                          return;
155.              }
156.              if(item < root->info)
157.              {
158.                          ptr = root->left;
159.                          save = root;
160.              }
161.              else
162.              {
163.                          ptr = root->right;
164.                          save = root;
166.              }
167.              while(ptr != NULL)
168.              {
169.                          if(item == ptr->info)
170.                          {
171.                                  *loc = ptr;
172.                                  *par = save;
173.                                  return;
174.                          }
175.                          else if(item > ptr->info)
176.                          {
177.                                  save = ptr;
178.                                  ptr = ptr->right;
179.                          }
180.                          else
```

```
181.                          {
182.                                  save = ptr;;
183.                                  ptr = ptr->left;
184.                          }
185.                  }
186.          *loc = NULL;
187.          *par = save;
188.  }
189.  void delnode(struct node **root,int item)
190.  {
191.          struct node *par,*loc,*t;
192.          search(*root,item,&par,&loc);
193.          if(loc == NULL)
194.          {
195.                  printf("Such a node does not exist");
196.                  return;
197.          }
198.          if(loc->left != NULL && loc->right != NULL)
199.                  caseb(root,&par,&loc);
200.          else
201.                  casea(root,&par,&loc);
202.          free(loc);
203.  }
204.  void casea(struct node **root, struct node **par, struct node **loc)
205.  {
206.          struct node *child;
207.          if((*loc)->left == NULL && (*loc)->right == NULL)
208.                  child = NULL;
209.          else if((*loc)->left != NULL)
210.                  child = (*loc)->left;
211.          else
212.                  child = (*loc)->right;
213.          if(*par != NULL)
214.          {
215.                  if(*loc == (*par)->left)
216.                          (*par)->left = child;
217.                  else
218.                          (*par)->right = child;
219.          }
220.          else
221.                  *root = child;
222.  }
223.  void caseb(struct node **root, struct node **par, struct node **loc)
224.  {
225.          struct node *suc, *parsuc, *ptr, *save;
226.          ptr = (*loc)->right;
```

```
227.            save = *loc;
228.            while(ptr->left != NULL)
229.            {
230.                    save = ptr;
231.                    ptr = ptr->left;
232.            }
233.            suc = ptr;
234.            parsuc = save;
235.            casea(root,&parsuc,&suc);
236.            if(*par != NULL)
237.            {
238.                    if((*par)->left == *loc)
239.                            (*par)->left = suc;
240.                    else
241.                            (*par)->right = suc;
242.            }
243.            else
244.                    *root = suc;
245.            suc->left = (*loc)->left;
246.            suc->right = (*loc)->right;
247.    }
248.    int count(struct node *root)
249.    {
250.            int cntl,cntr,cnt;
251.            if(root == NULL)
252.                    return(0);
253.    cntl = count(root->left);
254.            cntr = count(root->right);
255.            cnt = cntl+cntr+1;
256.            return(cnt);
257.    }
258.    int depth(struct node *root)
259.    {
260.            int depl,depr,dep;
261.            if(root == NULL)
262.                    return(0);
263.            depl = depth(root->left);
264.            depr = depth(root->right);
265.            if(depl>depr)
266.                    dep = depl+1;
267.            else
268.                    dep = depr+1;
269.            return(dep);
270.    }
271.    void traverse(struct node *root)
272.    {
```

```
273.              int ch;
274.              printf("\t\t  1.Traversing of Tree in Pre-Order.\n");
275.              printf("\t\t  2.Traversing of Tree in Post-Order.\n");
276.              printf("\t\t  3.Traversing of Tree in In-Order.\n");
277.              printf("\t\t  Enter Your Choice:- ");
278.              scanf("%d",&ch);
279.              clrscr();
280.              switch(ch)
281.                  {
282.                          case 1:
283.                                  printf("All The Nodes ( In Pre-Order ) Are:-
\n");
284.                                  pre_trav(root);
285.                                  break;
286.                          case 2:
287.                                  printf("All The Nodes ( In Post-Order ) Are:-
\n");
288.                                  post_trav(root);
289.                                  break;
290.                          case 3:
291.                                  printf("All The Nodes ( In In-Order ) Are:-
\n");
292.                                  in_trav(root);
293.                                  break;
294.                          default:
295.                                  printf("Wrong Choice !. Try Again. ");
296.                  }
297.      }
298.      void pre_trav(struct node *root)
299.      {
300.              if(root == NULL)
301.                      return;
302.              printf("%d\n",root->info);
303.              pre_trav(root->left);
304.              pre_trav(root->right);
305.      }
306.      void post_trav(struct node *root)
307.      {
308.              if(root == NULL)
309.                      return;
310.              post_trav(root->left);
311.              post_trav(root->right);
312.              printf("%d\n",root->info);
313.      }
314.      void in_trav(struct node *root)
315.      {
```

```
316.            if(root == NULL)
317.                    return;
318.            in_trav(root->left);
319.            printf("%d\n",root->info);
320.            in_trav(root->right);
321.    }
322.    void traverse2(struct node *root)
323.    {
324.            int ch;
325.            printf("\t\t  1.Traversing of Tree in Pre-Order.\n");
326.            printf("\t\t  2.Traversing of Tree in Post-Order.\n");
327.            printf("\t\t  3.Traversing of Tree in In-Order.\n");
328.            printf("\t\t  Enter Your Choice:- ");
329.            scanf("%d",&ch);
330.            clrscr();
331.            switch(ch)
332.                    {
333.                            case 1:
334.                                    printf("All The Nodes ( In Pre-Order ) Are:-
\n");
335.                                    pre_trav2(root);
336.                                    break;
337.                            case 2:
338.                                    printf("All The Nodes ( In Post-Order ) Are:-
\n");
339.    //                          post_trav2(root);
340.                                    break;
341.                            case 3:
342.                                    printf("All The Nodes ( In In-Order ) Are:-
\n");
343.                                    in_trav2(root);
344.                                    break;
345.                            default:
346.                                    printf("Wrong Choice !. Try Again. ");
347.                    }
348.    }
349.    void pre_trav2(struct node *root)
350.    {
351.            struct node *ptr;
352.            struct stack s1;
353.            s1.top = -1;
354.            push(&s1,NULL);
355.            ptr = root;
356.            while(ptr != NULL)
357.                    {
358.                            printf("%d\n",ptr->info);
```

```
359.                    if(ptr->right != NULL)
360.                            push(&s1,ptr->right);
361.                    if(ptr->left != NULL)
362.                            ptr = ptr->left;
363.                    else
364.                            ptr = pop(&s1);
365.            }
366.    }
367.    void in_trav2(struct node *root)
368.    {
369.            struct node *ptr;
370.            struct stack s1;
371.            s1.top = -1;
371.            push(&s1,NULL);
372.            ptr = root;
373.            while(ptr != NULL)
374.            {
375.                    push(&s1,ptr);
376.                    ptr = ptr->left;
377.            }
378.            ptr = pop(&s1);
379.            while(ptr != NULL)
380.            {
381.                    printf("%d\n",ptr->info);
382.                    if(ptr->right != NULL)
383.                    {
384.                            ptr = ptr->right;
385.                            while(ptr != NULL)
386.                            {
387.                                    push(&s1,ptr);
388.                                    ptr = ptr->left;
389.                            }
390.                            ptr = pop(&s1);
391.                    }
392.                    else
393.                            ptr = pop(&s1);
394.            }
396.    }
397.    void push(struct stack *p, struct node *item)
398.    {
399.            if(p->top == MAXSTK-1)
400.            {
401.                    printf("Stack is full");
402.                    return;
403.            }
404.            p->top++;
```

```
405.            p->info[p->top] = item;
406.    }
407.    struct node *pop(struct stack *p)
408.    {
409.            struct node * item;
410.            if(p->top == -1)
411.            {
412.                    printf("Stack is empty");
413.                    return (NULL);
414.            }
415.            item= p->info[p->top];
416.            p->top--;
417.            return (item);
418.    }
```

CHAPTER

∞ **9** ∞

(Graph)

Introduction-

Graph is another important non-linear data structure. This data structure is used to represent relationship between pairs of elements which are not necessarily hierarchical in nature.

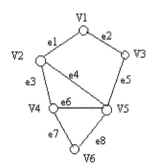

A graph G consists of a set V, whose members are called the vertices of G, together with a set E of pairs of distinct vertices from V.

These pairs are called the edges of G. If e1 = (v1,v2) is an edge with vertices v1 and v2, then v1 and v2 are said to lie on e1, and e1 is said to be incident with v1 and v2.

V = {v1,v2,v3,v4,v5,v6}   Vertices
E = {e1,e2,e3,e4,e5,e6,e7,e8}   Edges
e1 = (v1,v2)

Application of Graph :

Graph can be used in following areas-

- Cities and the highways connecting them form a graph.
- The components on a circuit board with the connections among them.
- An organic chemical compound can be considered a graph with the atoms as the vertices and the bonds between them as edges.
- The people living in a city can be regarded as the vertices of a graph with the relationship is acquainted with describing the edges.
- People working in a corporation form a directed graph with the relation "supervises" describing the edges.

Graph terms :

1. Directed Graph :

    If the pairs of a graph are ordered or edges represents a direction is called a directed graph. It is also called as Di-Graph.
    e1 = <v1,v2> It shows that e is a directed edge from v1 to v2.

2. Undirected Graph :

    If the pairs of a graph are not ordered or edges does not represents a direction is called a Undirected Graph.
    e1 = (v1,v2) It shows that e is a un-directed edge between v1 to v2.

3. Self Loop :

    An edge in which head and tail are same. An edge is a loop if it has identical endpoints i.e. if e=(v1,v1).

4. Incident :- if e1 = (v1,v2) then e1 is incident on v1 and v2.

5. Adjacent :- if e1 = (v1,v2) is a undirected edge then v1 and v2 are adjacent and if e1 = <v1,v2> is a directed edge then v1 is adjacent to v2 but v2 is not adjacent to v1.

6. Degree of a node :- No. of edges incidenting on a node.

7. In-degree of a node:- The number of edges in which a node is the head is called as the indegree of that node.

8. Out-degree of a node:- The number of edges in which a node is the tail is called as the outdegree of that node.

9. Isolated Vertex :-   Node of a degree zero.

10. Pendant Vertex :-   Node of a degree one.

11. Path :- Path is a sequence of vertex and edges such that no edge or vertex repeats in the path and each edge incidents on preceding and following vertices.
Path = v1 e1 v2 e2 v3 e3 v4 e4 v5

12. Cycle :- If first and last vertex is same is called as circuit or cycle.

13. Connected Graph :- If we can reach any node from any other node.

14. Disconnected Graph :- If it is not possible to reach some nodes from other nodes.

15. Strongly connected Graph :- A graph which is connected in case of undirected graph and if the same graph becomes directed then also it is connected it is called as strongly connected graph A directed graph G is said to be strongly connected, if for each pair u,v of vertices in G, if there exists a path from u to v, there must exist a path from v to u.

16. Weakly connected Graph :- A graph which is connected in case of undirected graph and if the same graph becomes directed then it is not connected it is called as weakly connected graph.

17. Tree Graph :- Tree is also a graph without any cycle. In tree there is a single path between two nodes. If there is n nodes tehn the number of edges will be n-1.—

18. Complete Graph :- A graph G is said to complete or fully connected if there is path from every vertex to every other vertex. A complete graph with n vertices will have n(n-1)/2 edges.

19. Weighted Graph :- A graph is said to weighted graph if every edge in the graph is assigned some data. The weight of the edge can be denoted by w(e), is a non-negative value that may be representing the cost of moving along that edge or distance between the vertices.

20. Source and Sink :- A vertex v1 is called a source if it has a outdegree greater than zero, but zero indegree. Similarly, a vertex v1 is called sink if it has indegree greater than zero, but zero outdegree.

22. Directed Acyclic Graph :- A directed graph G is a directed graph without any cycles. It is also called as DAG.

Max number of edges

Un-Directed Graph :-
$1 + 2 + 3 + \ldots\ldots\ldots N = N(N+1) / 2$ (including self loop)
$1 + 2 + 3 + \ldots\ldots\ldots N-1 = N(N-1) / 2$ (without self loop)

Directed Graph :-
N^2 (including self loop)
$N(N-1)$ (without self loop)

REPRESENTATION OF GRAPHS

There are two popular ways that are used to maintain a graph in a computer memory. These are

A. Sequential.
B. Linked List.

A. Sequential Representation

The graphs can be represented as matrices in sequential representation. There are two most common matrices. These are:

1. Adjacency.
2. Incidence.

1. The adjacency matrix is a sequence matrix with one row and one column for each vertex. The values of the matrix are either 0 or 1.

A value of 1 for row I and column j implies that edge eij exists between vi and vj vertices. A value of 0 implies that there is no edge between vertex vi and vj.

In other words we can say that if graph G consists of v1,v2,v3,....vn vertices then the adjacency matrix A = [aij] of the graph G is the n x n matrix.

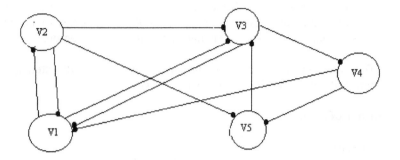

The adjacency matrix A for G is as follows:

	V1	v2	v3	v4	v5
V1	0	1	1	0	0
V2	1	0	1	0	1
v3	1	0	0	1	0
V4	1	0	0	0	1
V5	0	0	1	0	0

A =

2. The incidence matrix consists of a row for every vertex and a column for every edge. The values of the matrix are –1, 0 or 1. If the kth edge is (vi, vj), the kth column has a value 1 in the ith row, -1 in the jth row and 0 else where. For example, the incidence matrix I for the graph is as follows

	e1	e2	e3	e4	e5	e6	e7	e8	e9	e10
V1	1	1	-1	0	0	-1	0	-1	0	0
V2	-1	0	1	1	1	0	0	0	0	0
V3	0	-1	0	-1	0	1	1	0	0	-1
V4	0	0	0	0	0	0	-1	1	1	0
V5	0	0	0	0	-1	0	0	0	-1	1

I =

B. Adjacency List Representation

Although the adjacency list representation requires very less memory as compared to the adjacency matrix, the simplicity of adjacency matrix make it preferable when graphs are reasonably small.

V1	→	v2	→	v3		
V2	→	v1	→	v3	→	v5
V3	→	v1	→	v4		
V4	→	v1	→	v5		
V5	→	v3				

Graph Traversal-

In many problems we wish to investigate all the vertices in a graph in some systematic order, just as with binary trees we developed several systematic traversal methods.

In tree traversal, we had a root vertex with which we generally started but in graph we of tern do not have any one vertex singled out as special, and therefore the traversal may start at an arbitrary vertex.

Although there are many possible orders for visiting the vertices of the graph, two methods are of particular importance.

DFS –

Depth First Traversal :- DFS of a graph is same as preorder traversal of an ordered tree. Suppose that the traversal has just visited a vertex v, and let w0,w1,...,wk be the vertices adjacent to v. Then we shall next visit w0 and keep w1,....,wk waiting.

After visiting w0 we traverse all the vertices to which it is adjacent before returning to traverse w1,...,wk. DFS is naturally formulated as a recursive algorithm. In graph traversal two difficulties arises that cannot appear for tree traversal.

First, the graph may contain cycles, so out traversal algorithm may reach the same vertex a second time.

To prevent infinite recursion, we therefore introduce a Boolean-valued array visited, set visited[v] to TRUE before starting the recursion, and check the value of visited[w] before processing w.

Second the graph may not be connected, so the traversal algorithm may fail to reach all vertices from a single starting point. Hence enclose the action in a loop that runs through all vertices.

BFS –

Breadth first traversal :- BFS of a graph is same as level by level traversal of an ordered tree. If the traversal has just visited a vertex v, then it next visits all the vertices adjacent to v, putting the vertices adjacent to these in a waiting list to be traversed after all vertices adjacent to v have been visited. BFS can be implemented using a queue.

This algorithm executes a **depth-first search** on a graph G containing N nodes beginning at a starting node A.

1. Initialize all nodes to the ready state (STATUS = 1).
2. Push the starting node A onto STACK and change its status to the waiting state (STATUS = 2).
3. Repeat steps 4 and 5 until STACK is empty:
   4. Pop the top node N of STACK. Process N and change its status to the processed state (STACK = 3).
   5. Push onto STACK all the neighbors of N that are still in the ready state (STATUS = 1), and change their status to the waiting state (STATUS = 2).
   [End of Step 3 loop.]
6. Exit.

This algorithm executes a **breadth-first search** on a graph G containing N nodes beginning at a starting node A.

1. Initialize all nodes to the ready state (STATUS = 1).
2. Push the starting node A onto QUEUE and change its status to the waiting state (STATUS = 2).
3. Repeat steps 4 and 5 until QUEUE is empty:

   4. Remove the front node N of QUEUE. Process N and change its status to the processed state (STACK = 3).

5. Add to the rear of QUEUE all the neighbors of N that are still in the ready state (STATUS = 1), and change their status to the waiting state (STATUS = 2).
   [End of Step 3 loop.]
6. Exit.

Adjacency List is:

V1	→	v2	→	v3		
V2	→	v1	→	v3	→	v5
V3	→	v1	→	v4		
V4	→	v1	→	v5		
V5	→	v3				

DFS
    V1,V2,V3,V4,V5
BFS
    V1,V2,V3,V5,V4

DEGREE (NODE, NEXT, ADJ, START, DEST, LINK, INDEG, OUTDEG)
This procedure finds the indegree INDEG and outdegree OUTDEG of each node in the graph G in memory.

1. [Initialize arrays INDEG AND OUTDEG.]
    (a) Set PTR:= START.
    (b) Repeat while PTR ≠ NULL: [Traverse node list.]
        (i) Set INDEG[PTR]:= 0 and OUTDEG[PTR]:= 0.
        (ii) Set PTR:= NEXT[PTR].
    [End of step (b) loop.]
2. Set PTRA:= START.
3. REPEAT Steps 4 to 6 while PTRA ≠ NULL: [Traverses node list.]
4.   Set PTRB:= ADJ[PTRA].
5.   Repeat while PTRB ≠ NULL: [Traverses list of neighbors.]
        (a) Set OUTDEG[PTRA]:= OUTDEG[PTRA] + 1 and
          INDEG[DEST[PTRB]]:= INDEG[DEST[PTRB]] + 1.
        (b) Set PTRB:= LINK[PTRB].
    [End of inner loop using pointer PTRB.]
6.   Set PTRA:= NEXT[PTRA].
  [End of step 3 outer loop using the pointer PTRA.]
7. Return.

SPANNING TREE-

A tree T is called a spanning tree of a connected graph G if T has the same nodes as G and all the edges of T are contained among the edges of G. It can not contain a cycle.

MINIMUM COST SPANNING TREE-

A connected weighted graph G is called as a spanning tree T for G such that the sum of weights of the tree edges in T is as small as possible. Such a tree is called a minimum spanning tree and represents the cheapest way of connecting all the nods in G.

There are a number of techniques for creating a minimum spanning tree for a weighted graph. The first of these, Prim's algorithm, discovered independently by Prim and Dijkstra, is very much like Dijkstra's algorithm for finding shortest paths.

An arbitrary node is chosen initially as the tree root(nothe than in an undirected graph and its spanning tree, any node can be considered the root and the nodes adjacent to it as its sons). The nodes of the graph are then appended to the tree one at a time until all nodes of the graph are included. The node of the graph added to the tree at each point is that node adjacent to a node of the tree by an arc of minimum weight. The arc of minimum weight becomes a tree arc connecting the new node to the tree. When all the nodes of the graph have been added to the tree, a minimum spanning tree has been constructed for the graph

Procedure MIN_SPANNING_TREE (G, T, N)

This algorithm finds a minimum spanning tree T of a weighted graph G

Step 1. Order all the edges of G according to increasing weights.
Step 2. Initialize T to be a graph consisting of the same nodes as G and no edges.
Step 3. Repeat the following N-1 times, where N is the number of nodes in G
         Add to T an
         edge E of G with minimum weight such that E does not form a cycle in T.
         [End of loop.]
Step 4. Exit.

Warshall's Algorith to find the Path matrix.

A directed graph G with M nodes is maintained in memory by its adjacency matrix A. This algorithm finds the (Boolean) path matrix P of the graph G.

1.   [Initialize P.]
        Repeat steps for I:= 1 to M:
                Repeat steps for J:= 1 to M:
                        If A[I,J] = 0, then:
                                Set P[I,J]:= 0.
                        Else:
                                Set P[I,J]:= 1.
                        [End of Is structure.]
                [End of J loop.]
        [End of I loop.]
2.   [Updates P.]
        Repeat steps for k:= 1 to M:
                Repeat steps for I:= 1 to M:
                        Repeat steps for J:= 1 to M:
                                Set P[I,J]:= P[I,J] and (P[I,K] or P[K,J]).
                        [End of J loop.]
                [End of I loop.]
        [End of K loop.]
3.   Exit

Warshall's Algorith to find the shortest Path matrix.

A weighted graph G with M nodes is maintained in memory by its weight matrix W. This algorithm finds a matrix Q such that Q[I,J] is the length of a shortest path from node V1 to node V2.

INFINITY is a very large number, and MIN is the minimum value function.

1.   [Initialize Q.]
       Repeat steps for I:= 1 to M:
              Repeat steps for J:= 1 to M:
                     If W[I,J] = 0, then:
                            Set Q[I,J]:= INFINITY.
                     Else:
                            Set Q[I,J]:= W[I,J].
                  [End of Is structure.]
              [End of J loop.]
       [End of I loop.]
2.   [Updates Q.]
       Repeat steps for k:= 1 to M:
              Repeat steps for I:= 1 to M:
                     Repeat steps for J:= 1 to M:
                            Set Q[I,J]:= MIN(Q[I,J] , Q[I,K] + Q[K,J]).
                  [End of J loop.]
              [End of I loop.]
       [End of K loop.]
3.   Exit

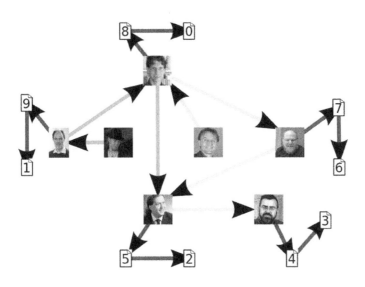

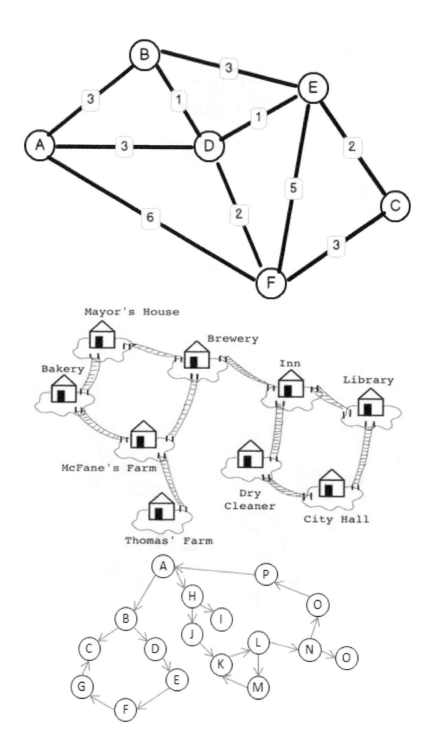

CHAPTER
∞ **10** ∞
(HASHING)

Introduction-

In all the search algorithms considered so far, the location of the item is determined by a sequence of comparisons. In each case, a data item sought is repeatedly compared with items in certain locations of the data structure. However, the number of actual comparison depends on the data structure and the search algorithm used. For example

- In an array and linked list, the linear search requires O(N) comparisons.
- In a sorted array, the binary search requires $O(\log_2 N)$ comparisons.
- In a binary search tree, search requires $O(\log_2 N)$ comparisons.

However, there are some applications that require search to be performed in constant time i.e. O(1). Ideally, it may not be possible, but still we can achieve a performance very close to it. And this is possible using a data structure known as *hash table*.

A *hash table*, in basic sense, is a generalized of the simpler notion of an ordinary array. Directly addressing into an array makes it possible to access any data element of the array in O(1) time. For example, if a[1...100] is an ordinary array, then the nth data element, $1<=n<=100$, can be directly accessed as a[n]. However, direct accessing is applicable only when we can allot an array that has one position for every possible key. In addition, direct addressing suffers from the following problems:

Hashing, Hash Data Structure and Hash Table-

Hashing is the process of mapping large amount of data item to a smaller table with the help of a hashing function. The essence of hashing is to facilitate the next level searching method when compared with the linear or binary search.

The advantage of this searching method is its efficiency to hand vast amount of data items in a given collection (i.e. collection size).

Due to this hashing process, the result is a Hash data structure that can store or retrieve data items in an average time disregard to the collection size.

Hash Table is the result of storing the hash data structure in a smaller table which incorporates the hash function within itself. The Hash Function primarily is responsible to map between the original data item and the smaller table itself.

Here the mapping takes place with the help of an output integer in a consistent range produced when a given data item (any data type) is provided for storage and this output integer range determines the location in the smaller table for the data item.

In terms of implementation, the hash table is constructed with the help of an array and the indices of this array are associated to the output integer range.

WHAT IS HASHING , HASHTABLE, HASH FUNCTION AND ITS COLLISION RESOLUTION STRATEGIES-

Hashing is the technique used for performing almost constant time search in case of insertion, deletion and find operation. Taking a very simple example of it, an array with its index as key is the example of hash table.

So each index (key) can be used for accessing the value in a constant search time. This mapping key must be simple to compute and must helping in identifying the associated value.

Function which helps us in generating such kind of key-value mapping is known as Hash Function.

Hash Table Example :

Here, we construct a hash table for storing and retrieving data related to the citizens of a county and the social-security number of citizens are used as the indices of the array implementation (i.e. key). Let's assume that the table size is 12, therefore the hash function would be Value modulus of 12.

Hence, the Hash Function would equate to:
(sum of numeric values of the characters in the data item) %12
Note! % is the modulus operator

Let us consider the following social-security numbers and produce a hashcode:
120388113D => 1+2+0+3+8+8+1+1+3+13=40
Hence, (40)%12 => Hashcode=4

310181312E => 3+1+0+1+8+1+3+1+2+14=34
Hence, (34)%12 => Hashcode=10

041176438A => 0+4+1+1+7+6+4+3+8+10=44
Hence, (44)%12 => Hashcode=8

Therefore, the Hashtable content would be as follows:

0:empty
1:empty
2:empty
3:empty
4:occupied Name:Drew Smith SSN:120388113D
5:empty
6:empty
7:empty
8:occupied Name:Andy Conn SSN:041176438A
9:empty
10:occupied Name:Igor Barton SSN:310181312E
11:empty

1. If the total number of possible keys is very large, it my not be possible to allocate an array of that size because of the memory available in the system or the applications software does not permit it.

2. If the actually number of keys is very small as compared to total number of possible keys, lot of space in the array will be wasted.

Therefore, in practice, when the number of keys actually stored is small relative to total number of possible keys, a hash table becomes more effective since a hash table typically uses an array of size proportional to the number of keys actually stored. Further, instead of using the key as array index directly, the array index is computed from the key.

HASH TABLE:

A hash table is a data structure in which the location of a data item is determined directly as a function of the data item itself rather than by a sequence of comparisons. Under ideal condition, the time required to locate a data item in a hash table is $O(1)$ i.e. it is constant and does nor depend on the number of data items stored.

When the set of k of keys stored is much smaller than the universe U of all possible keys, a hash table requires much less storage space than a direct-address table. In direct-address table, an element with key k is stored in slot k, whereas this element is stored in slot h(k) that is a hash function h is used to compute the slot from the key k. Here, the hash function h maps the universe U of keys into the slots of a hash table.

This process of mapping keys to appropriate slots in a hash table is known as hashing.

The main flaw of this beautiful idea is that two or more keys may hash to the same slot, which lead to the condition called collision. Ideally it would have been nice if the collision could be avoided by carefully choosing a hash function.

But in practice it is not possible to avoid collision irrespective of the nature of the hash function. Therefore, in these circumstances the best solution is to minimize the number of collisions and device a scheme to resolve these collisions if they occur.

The following schemes for resolving collisions:-

1. Collision resolution by separating chaining.
2. Collision resolution by open addressing.

Hash function:

A hash function h is simply a mathematical formula that manipulates the key in some form to compute the index for this key in the hash table. For example a hash function can divide the key by some number usually the size of the hash table and return remainder as the index for the key.

The process of mapping keys to appropriate slots in a hash table is known as hashing.

The main considerations while choosing a particular hash function h are

1. It should be possible to compute it efficiently.
2. It should distribute the keys uniformly across the hash table i.e. it should keep the number of collisions as minimum as possible.

Different hash functions:-

1.   **Division method:-**

In division method, key k to be mapped into one of the m slots in the has-table is divided by m and the remainder of this division is taken as index into the has-table
That is the hash function is $h(k) = k \bmod m$
Since it requires only a single division operation, hashing is quite fast.
When using the division method, certain values of m should be avoided.
It has been proved in literature that good values for m are prime values not too close to exact power of 2.

2.   **Mid square method:-**

The mid square method also operates in two steps. In the first step, the square of the key value k is taken. In the second step, the hash value is obtained by deleting digits from ends of the squared value i.e. k^2. It is important to note that same position of k^2 must be used for all keys. Thus, the hash function is

$H(k) = s$ where s is obtained by deleting digits from both sides of k^2.

3.   **Folding method:-**

The folding method also operates in two steps. In the first step, the key value k is divided into number of parts, k1, k2, k3,... , kr, where each part has the same number of digits except the last part, which can have lesser digits.

In the second step, these parts are added together and the hash value is obtained by ignoring the last carry, if any. For example, if the hash table has 1000 slots, each part will have three digits, and the sum of these parts after ignoring the last carry will also be three-digit number in the range of 0 to 999.

K = 9234   parts are 92,35 sum is 127 h(k) = 27

Resolving Collisions:-
A collision is a phenomena that occurs when more than one key maps to same slot in the hash table. Though we can keep collisions to a certain minimum level, but we cannot eliminate them altogether. Then we need some mechanism to handle them.

1.Collision resolutions by separating chaining:-

In this scheme, all the elements whose keys hash to the same hash table contains a pointer to the head of the linked list of all the elements that hash to value i. If there is no such element that hash to value i, the slot i contains NULL value.

2.Collision resolution by open addressing:-

In the open addressing scheme all the elements of the dynamic set are stored in the hash-table itself. That is each entry of the hash-table either contains the element of the dynamic set or some sentinel value to indicate that slot is free. In case if it is known that no key can be negative, value −1 can be taken as sentinel value.

In order to insert a key in a hash table under this scheme, if the slot to which key is hashed is free then the element is stored at that slot. In case the slot is filled, then other slots are examined systematically, in the forward direction, to find the free slot. If no such slot is found the overflow conditions occurs.

In case of searching, the element stored in the slot to which key is hashed is compared with element to be searched and if it matches search operation succeeds. If it does not match then other slots are examined systematically, in the forward direction, to find the slot contained containing the element under consideration. If no such slot is found then search ends in a failure.

In each case the process of examining the slots in the hash table is called probing.

1. Linear Probing:-

The linear probing uses the following hash functions
$h(k) = [h(k) + i] \bmod m$ where is the probe number.

Linear probing is very easy to implement, but is suffers from a problem known as primary clustering. Here by a cluster we mean a block of occupied slots and primary clustering refers to many such blocks separated by free slots.

Therefore, once clusters are formed there are more chances that subsequent insertions will also end up in one of the clusters and thereby increasing the size of cluster. Thus increasing the number of probes required to find a free slot, and hence worsening the performance further.

To avoid problem of primary clustering, some remedies are suggested. Two of them are quadratic probing and double hashing.

A. Quadratic probing:-

The Quadratic probing uses the following hash functions
$h(k) = [h(k)], [h(k) + i], [h(k) + i^2], \ldots \bmod m$ where is the probe number.

2. **Double hashing:-**

Double hashing is one of the best methods available for open addressing because the permutations produced have many of the characteristics of randomly chosen permutations.

Double hashing uses a hash function of the form
$H(k) = [h(k) + i*h'(k)] \mod m$ where i is the probe number.

Direct Address Tables-

If we have a collection of **n** elements whose keys are unique integers in $(1,m)$, where **m** >= **n**, then we can store the items in a *direct address* table, **T[m]**, where **T$_i$** is either empty or contains one of the elements of our collection.

Searching a direct address table is clearly an **O(1)** operation:
for a key, **k**, we access **T$_k$,**

- if it contains an element, return it,

- if it doesn't then return a NULL.

There are two constraints here:

1. the keys must be unique, and

2. the range of the key must be severely bounded.

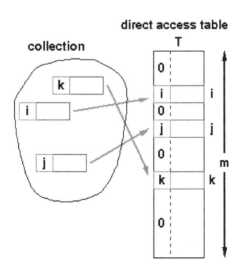

direct access table

If the keys are not unique, then we can simply construct a set of **m** lists and store the heads of these lists in the direct address table. The time to find an element matching an input key will still be **O(1)**.

However, if each element of the collection has some other distinguishing feature (other than its key), and if the maximum number of duplicates is $n_{dup}{}^{max}$, then searching for a specific element is $O(n_{dup}{}^{max})$.

If duplicates are the exception rather than the rule, then $n_{dup}{}^{max}$ is much smaller than **n** and a direct address table will provide good performance. But if $n_{dup}{}^{max}$ approaches **n**, then the time to find a specific element is **O(n)** and a tree structure will be more efficient.

The range of the key determines the size of the direct address table and may be too large to be practical. For instance it's not likely that you'll be able to use a direct address table to store elements which have arbitrary 32-bit integers as their keys for a few years yet!

Direct addressing is easily generalised to the case where there is a function,

h(k) => (1,m)

which maps each value of the key, **k**, to the range (1,m). In this case, we place the element in **T[h(k)]** rather than **T[k]** and we can search in **O(1)** time as before.

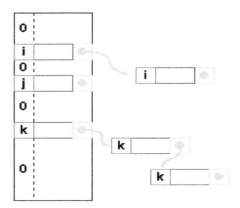

Q1.   What is recursion? How are values computed for a recursively designed fuction? Explain with an example clearly name the data structure required and operations on the data structure.

CHAPTER
∞ **11** ∞
(MISC. TOPICS)

Introduction-

Recursion:

In mathematics and computer science, recursion means self-reference. A recursive function, therefore, is a function whose definition is based upon itself. In other words, a function containing either a call statement to itself or a call statement toanother function that may result in a call statement back to the original function, then that function is called a recursive function.

It is an important concept in computer science and is convinient for a variety of problems that would be difficult to solve using for, while and do-while loops. Recursion functions can be directly implemented in any language. Many algorithms can be best described in terms of recursion.
It must have following properties:

1. Base criteria - There must be certain criteria called base criteria, for which the function does not call itself.

2. Closer to base criteria – Each time the function does call itself (directly or indirectly) it must be closer to the base criteria i.e. it uses an argument(s) smaller than the one it was given.

When we define a function recursively then the values can be computed by using following steps-

1. If a terminating condition encountered then the control exit from this function and follow backtracking. Control jumps to the previous values which were stored in the stack.

2. If a recursive statement is cncountered then the current values are stored in a stack and a new set of values are computed and a new copy of the same function gets called. This process continues until terminating condition is encountered.

Example:-

Let us calculate 3! Using the recursive definition. It requires 7 steps It uses the formula that n! = n * (n-1)!

1.   3! = 3 * 2!
2.   2! = 2 * 1!
3.   1! = 1 * 0!
4.   0! = 1
5.   1! = 1 * 1 = 1
6.   2! = 2 * 1 = 2
7.   3! = 3 * 2 = 6

Expaination :

Step 1 In this step to calculate 3! We must postpone evaluating 3! Until we evaluate 2!.

Step 2 In this step to calculate 2! We must postpone evaluating 2! Until we evaluate 1!.

Step 3 In this step to calculate 1! We must postpone evaluating 1! Until we evaluate 0!.

Step 4.This step does not requires recursion because factorial 0 can be computed directly i.e.1

Step 5-7 In these steps we backtrack from 0! To 1!, 1! To 2! And finally 2! To find 3! This bactracking is indicated by the reverse indentation.

FACTORIAL(N, FACT)
This procedure calulates the factorial of N recursivedly and assign the result in FACT.

Step 1. If N=0 Then Set FACT := 1, and Return.
Step 2   Call FACTORIAL(N-1, FACT) [Recursive Call]
Step 3   Set FACT := N * FACT
Step 4   Return.

Dangling Pointer:-

When we free a pointer by calling the function free(p) then the storage for *p is freed but the value of p is left unchanged. This means that a reference to *p becomes illegal, there may be no way of detecting the illegality. The value of p is a valid address and the object at that address of the proper type may be used as the value of *p. P is called a dangling pointer.

Compaction:-

Once the memory locations of a given systems have been marked appropriately, the collection phase may begin. The purpose of this phase is to return to available memory all those locations that were previously garbage (not used by any program but unavailable to any user). It is easy to pass through memory sequentially, examine each node in turn and return unmarked nodes to available storage.

Tries:-

A digital search tree need not be implemented as a binary tree. Instead, each node in the tree can contain *m* pointers, corresponding to the *m* possible symbol in each position of the key.

Thus, if the keys were numeric, there would be 10 pointers in a node, and if strictly alphbetic, there would 26. (There might also be an extra pointer corresponding to *eok*, or a flag with each pointer indicating that it pointed to a record rather than to a tree node.)

A pointer in a node is associated with a particular symbol value based on its position in the node; that is, the first pointer corresponds to the lowest symbol value, the second pointer to the second lowest, and so forth.

It is therefore unnecessary to keep the symbol values themselves in the tree. The number of nodes that must be accessed to find a particular key is log *mn*. A digital search tree implemented in this way is called a **trie**(from the word retrieval).

A trie is useful when the set of keys is dense, so that most of the pointer in each node are used. When the key set is spare, a trie wastes a large amount of space with large nodes that are mostly empty. If the set of keys in trie is known in advance and does not change, there are a number of techniques for minmizing the space requiirements.

One technique is to establish a different order in which the symbols of a key are used for searching (so that, for example, the third symbol of the argument key might be used to access the appropriate pointer in the trie root, the first symbol in level 1 nodes, and so forth.) Another technique is to allow trie nodes to overlap each other, so that occupied pointers of one node overlay empty pointers of another.

Greatest common divisor:-

```
#include<stdio.h>
#include<conio.h>
int gcd(int, int);
void main()
{
        int n,m;
        int ans;
        clrscr();
        printf("\n Enter two integer numbers");
        scanf("%d %d",&n,&m);
        ans = gcd(n,m);
        printf("GCD of %d and %d is %d",n,m,ans);
        getch();
}
int gcd(int n, int m)
{
        if(n >= m && n%m == 0)
                return(m);
        else
                return gcd(m,n%m);
}
```

Pattern Matching:-

P and T are strings with lengths R and S, respectively, and are stored as arrays with one character per elemet. This algorithm finds the INDEX of P in T.

1.   [Initialize] Set K:=1 and MAX:= S - R +1.
2.   Repeat Steps 3 to 5 while K<=MAX:
3.   Repeat for L:= 1 to R: [Tests each character of P.]
                        If P[L] ≠ T[K+L-1], then Go to Step 5.
                [End of if structure.]
4.   [Success.] Set INDEX := K, and Exit.
5.   Set K:= K+ 1.
        [End of Step 2 outer loop.]
6.   [Failure] Set INDEX := 0.
7.   Exit.

```c
/* Determinant */
#include<stdio.h>
#include<conio.h>
#define MAXROW 4
#define MAXCOL 4
int det_mat(int [][MAXCOL],int,int);
void main()
{
        int mat[MAXROW][MAXCOL]={0};
        int r,c,i,j,sum;
        clrscr();
        printf("Enter dimension of matrix");
        scanf("%d%d",&r,&c);

        /*Input Matrix */
        for(i=0;i<r;i++)
                for(j=0; j<c;j++)
                {
                        printf("Enter element %d %d", i+1, j+1);
                        scanf("%d",&mat[i][j]);
                }
        sum = det_mat(mat,r,c);

        printf("%d",sum);
        getch();
}
int det_mat(int mat[][MAXCOL], int r, int c)
{
        int i,j,k,sign,sum,a;
        int mat2[MAXROW][MAXCOL]={0};

        sign = 1;
        sum = 0;

        if(c == 1)
                return(mat[0][0]);

        for(i=0 ; i<c; i++,sign *= -1)
        {
                for(j=1; j<r; j++)
                {
                        for(k=0; k<c; k++)
                        {
                                if(k == i)
                                        continue;
```

```
                    if(k>i)
                            mat2[j-1][k-1]=mat[j][k];
                else
                            mat2[j-1][k]=mat[j][k];

            }
        }

        sum = sum + mat[0][i] * sign * det_mat(mat2,r-1,c-1);
    }
    return sum;
}
```

Bounded Queue:-

Defination:- A queue limited to a fixed number of item.

Skiplist Representation:-

A search in an n-element dictionary that is represented as a sorted chain requires up to n element comparisons. The number of comparisons can be reduced to n/2+1 if we keep a pointer to the middle element.

Now to search for an element, we first compare with the middle one. If we are looking for a smaller element, we need search only the left half of the sorted chain. If we are looking for a larger element, we need compare only the right half of the chain.

Example:-

Consider the seven element sorted chain of fig(a). The sorted chain has been augmented by a head and tail node. The number inside a node is its value. A search of this chain may involve up to seven element comparison.

We can reduce this worst case number of comparisons to four by keeping a pointer to the middle element and then, depending on the outcome, compare with either the left or right half of the chain. If we are looking for an element with value 26, then we begin by comparing 26 with the middle value 40. Since 26< 40, we need not search to the right of 40. if we are searching for an element with value 75, then we can limit the search to the element that follow 40.

We can reduce the worst case number of element comparison by keeping pointers to the middle elements of each half as in fig (c). In this fig we have three chains. The levels 0 chain is essentially that of fig (a) and include all seven elements of the dictionary.

The level 1 chain includes the second, fourth, and sixth elements while the level 2 chain includes only the fourth element. To search for an element with value30, we begin with a comparisons against the middle elements.

This element is found in O(1) time using the level 2 chain. Since 30<40, the search continues by examining the middle element of the left half. This element is also found in O(1) time using the level 1 chain. Since 30>24, we continue the search by dropping into level 0 chain and comparing with the next element in this chain.

As another example, Consider an example, the search for an element with value 77. The first comparison is with 40. since the 77>40, we drop into the level 1 chain and compare with the element (75) in this chain that comes just after 40. since 77>75, we drop into the level 0 chain and compare with the element (80) in this chain that comes just after 75.

At this time we know that 77 is not in the dictionary. Using the three chain structure of fig (c), we can perform all searches using the most three comparisons. The Three chain structure allows us to perform a binary search in the sorted chain.

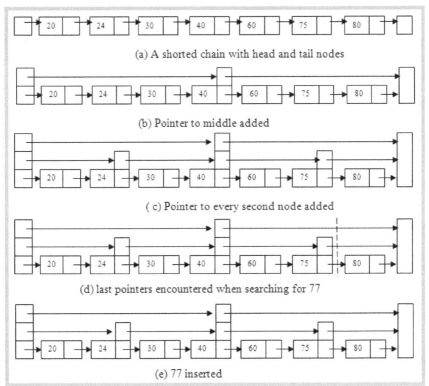

(a) A shorted chain with head and tail nodes

(b) Pointer to middle added

(c) Pointer to every second node added

(d) last pointers encountered when searching for 77

(e) 77 inserted

For general n, the level 0 chain includes all elements, the level 1 chain includes every second elements; the level 2 chain every fourth element; and the level i chain every 2^i th element.

We shall say that an element is a level i element iff it is the chains for levels 0 through i and it is not on the level i+1 chain in figure (c) 40 is the only level 2 element; 24 and 75 are the level 1 elements; and 20, 30, 60 and 80 are the level 0 elements.

We shall use the term **skip list** to refer to a structure in figure c. In such a structure we have a hierarchy of chains. The level 0 chain is a sorted chain of all elements.

The level 1 chain is also a sorted chain that is comprised of some subset of the elements on the level 0 chain. In general, the level i chain comprises a subset of the elements in the level i-1 chain. The skiplist of figure (c) has a very structure in that the level i chain comprises every other element of the level i-1 chain.

Unrolled Linklist:-

In computer programming, an **unrolled linked list** is a variation on the linked list which stores multiple elements in each node. It can drastically increase cache performance, while decreasing the memory overhead associated with storing list metadata such as references.

Overview:-
A typical unrolled linked list node looks like this:
record node
{
    node next   *// reference to next node in list*
    int numElements *// number of elements in this node, up to maxElements*
    array elements *// an array of numElements elements, with space*
                   // allocated for maxElements elements
}

Each node holds up to a certain maximum number of elements, typically just large enough so that the node fills a single cache line or a small multiple thereof. A position in the list is indicated by both a reference to the node and a position in the elements array. It's also possible to include a *previous* pointer for an unrolled doubly-linked linked list.

To insert a new element, we simply find the node the element should be in and insert the element into the elements array, incrementing numElements. If the array is already full, we first insert a new node either preceding or following the current one and move half of the elements in the current node into it.

To remove an element, similarly, we simply find the node it is in and delete it from the elements array, decrementing numElements.

If numElements falls below maxElements ÷ 2 then we pull elements from adjacent nodes to fill it back up to this level.

If both adjacent nodes are too low, we combine it with one adjacent node and then move some values into the other. This is necessary to avoid wasting space.

Another advantage of unrolled linked lists is that they perform a number of operations, typically associated with arrays, much more quickly than ordinary linked lists.

Associative array:-

An **associative array** is an abstract data type composed of a collection of keys and a collection of values, where each key is associated with one value.

The operation of finding the value associated with a key is called a *lookup* or indexing, and this is the most important operation supported by an associative array. The relationship between a key and its value is sometimes called a mapping or binding.

For example, if the value associated with the key "ajay" is 7, we say that our array *maps* "ajay" to 7. Associative arrays are very closely related to the mathematical concept of a function with a finite domain.

From the perspective of a programmer using an associative array, it can be viewed as a generalization of an array:

The operations that are usually defined for an associative array are:

+ **Add**: Bind a new key to a new value.

+ **Reassign**: Bind an old key to a new value.

+ **Remove**: Unbind a key from a value and remove the key from the key set.

+ **Lookup**: Find the value (if any) that is bound to a key .

Spanning Tree:-

There is a common problem associated with weighted graphs that of finding a minimal spanning tree for each connected component. A spanning tree for an undirected graph G is a graph T consisting of the nodes of G together with enough edges from G such that:

1.   There is a path between each pair of nodes in T.
2.   There are no simple cycle in T.

If a graph G=(VE) contains N nodes, then the spanning tree for that graph contains N-1 edges. The edges of spanning tree are subset of E.

In general, it is possible to construct different spanning trees for a graph, G. For any spanning tree, we could pick any node as root that would provide a parent-child relationship for the nodes connected by each node.

A "minimal spanning tree" for a weighted graph G is a spanning tree such that the sum of its weights is less than or equal to the sum of its heights of every other spanning tree for G. That is in a minimal spanning tree the sum of weights of the edges is as small as possible.

PRIM'S ALGORITHM for Minimum Spanning Tree:-

The algorithm due to prim builds up a minimum spanning tree by adding edges to form a sequence of expanding sub-trees. The sequence of sub-trees is represented by the pair(V_T, E_T), where V_T and E_T respectively represent the set of vertices and the set of edges of a sub-tree in the sequence.

Initially, the sub-tree in the sequence, consists of just a single vertex which is selected arbitrarily from the set V of vertices of the given graph. The sub-tree is build up iteratively by adding an edge that has minimum weight among the remaining edges and which at the same time, does not form a cycle with the earlier selected edges.

Example:

Let us explain through the following example how Prim's algorithm finds a minimal spanning tree of a given graph. Let us consider the following graph:
Initially
V_T=(a)
E_T=ϕ

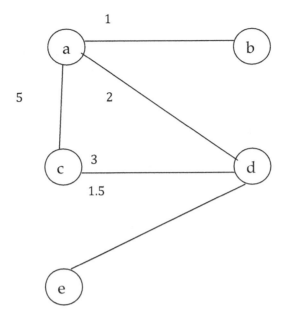

In the first iteration the edge having weight which is the minimum of the weights of the edges having a as one of its vertices is chosen. In this case, the edge ab with weight 1 is chosen out of the edges ab, ac and ad of weights respectively 1, 5 and 2. thus, after First iteration, we have the given graph with chosen edges in bold and V_T and E_T as follow:

V_T=(a,b)
E_T=((a,b))

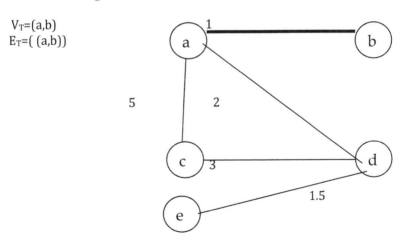

In the next iteration, out of the edges, not chosen earlier and not making a cycle with earlier chosen edge and having either a or b as one of its vertices, the edges with minimum weight is chosen. In this case the vertex b does not have any edge originating out of it. In such cases, if required, weight of a not having any edge taken as ∞.Thus choice is restricted to two edges viz. ad and ac respectively of weight 2 and 5. Hence in the next iteration the edge ad is chosen. Hence after second iteration. We have the given graph with chosen edges and V_T and E_T as follows: $V_T=(a,b,d)$

$E_T=(\ (a,b),\ (a,d))$

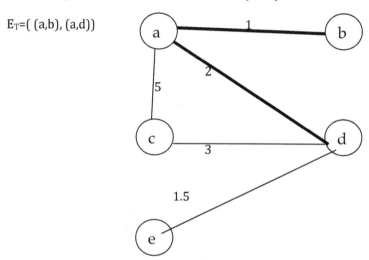

In the next iteration, out of the edges, not chosen earlier and not making a cycle with earlier chosen edges and having either a, b or d as one of its vertices, the edge with minimum weight is chosen. Thus choice is restricted to edges ac, dc and de with weights respectively 5, 3, 1.5. the edge de with weight 1.5 is selected. Hence, after third iteration we have the given graph with chosen edges and V_T and E_T as follow:

$V_T=(a,b,d,\ e)$
$E_T=(\ (a,b),\ (a,d)\ (d,e))$

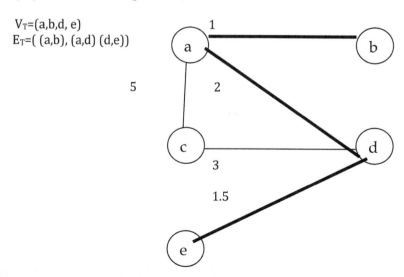

In the next iteration, out of the edges, not chosen earlier and not making a cycle with earlier chosen and having either a, b, d or e as one of its vertices, the edge with minimum weight is chosen.

Thus, choice is restricted to edges dc and ac with weights respectively 3 and 5. Hence the edge dc with weight 3 is chosen. Thus, after fourth iteration, we have the given graph with chosen edges and V_T and E_T as follows:

V_T=(a,b,d, e, c)
E_T=((a,b), (a,d) (d, e) (d, c))

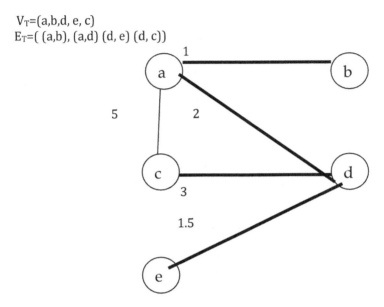

At this stage, it can be easily seen that each of the vertices, is on some chosen edge and the chosen edges form a tree.

ALGORITHM Spanning Prim's (G, E_T)

The algorithm constructs a minimum spanning tree for which the input is a weighted connected graph G=(V, T). The output is the set of edges, to be denoted by E_T, which together constitute a minimum spanning tree of the given graph G for the pair of vertices that are not adjacent in the graph to each other, can be given the label ∞ indicating "infinite" distance between the pair of vertices.

The set of vertices of the required tree is initialized with the vertex V_0.
set V_T:={v_0}.
set E_T:=φ.   [initially E_T is empty.]
[let N=number of vertices of vertices in V.]
Repeat steps for I:=1 to N -1:

Find a minimum weight edge $\underline{e}=(v^1, u^1)$ among all the edges such that v^1 is in V_T and u^1 is in $V-V_T$.

$V_T \leftarrow V_T\{u^1\}$

$E_T = E_T \cup \{\underline{e}\}$
[End of loop.]
Return.

Krushkal's Algorithm of Minimum spanning tree:-

Now we discuss the method of finding minimal spanning tree of a given weighted graph, which is suggested by Kruskal. In this method, the emphasis is on the choice of edges of minimum weight from amongst all the available edges, of course, subject to the condition that chosen edges do not form a cycle.

The connectivity of the chosen edges, at any stage, in the form of a subtree, which was emphasized in Prim's algorithm, is not essential.

We briefly describe the Krushal's algorithm to find the minimal spanning tree of a given weighted and connected graph, as follow:

(i)   first of all, order all the weights of the edges in increasing order. Then repeat the following two steps till a set of edges is selected containing all the vertices of the given graphs.

(ii)   Chosen an edges having the weight which is the minimum of the weights of the edges not selected so far.

(iii)   If the new edge forms a cycle with any subset of the earlier selected edges, then drop it, else, add the edge to the set of selected edges.

We illustrate the krushal's algorithm through the following:

Example 1:

Let us consider the following graph, for which the minimal spanning tree is required.

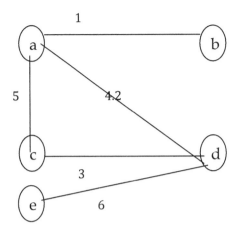

Let E_g denote the set of edges of the graph that are chosen upto some stage. According to the step (i) above, the weights of the edges are arranged in increasing order as the set

{1, 3, 4.2, 5, 6}

In the first iteration, the edge(a,b) is chosen which is of weight 1, the minimum of all the weights of the edges of the graph.

As single edge do not form a cycle, therefore, the edge(a, b) is selected, so that $E_{g=((a,b))}$

After first iteration, the graph with selected edges in bold is as shown below:

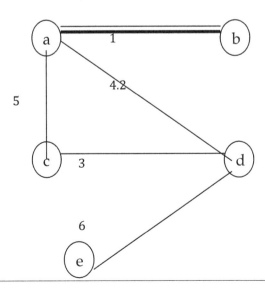

Second iteration-

Next the edges (c,d) is of weight 3, miminum for the remaining edges. Also edges (a,b) and (c, d) do not form a cycle, as shown below: Therefore (c,d) is selected so that,

$E_{g=((a,b), (c, d))}$

Thus, after second iteration, the graph with selected edges in bold is as shown below:

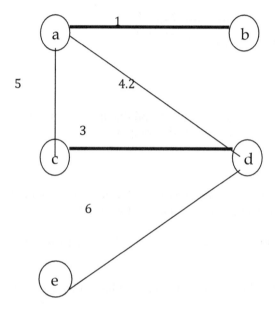

It may be observed that the selected edges do not form a connected subgraph or subtree of the given graph.

Third iteration-

Next, the edges (a,b) is of weight 4.2, the minimum for the remaining edges. Also the edges in E_g alongwith the edge (a,b) do not form a cycle.

Therefore (a,d) is selected so that new $E_{g=((a,b), (c, d), (a,d))}$. Thus after third iteration, the graph with selected edges in bold is as shown below:

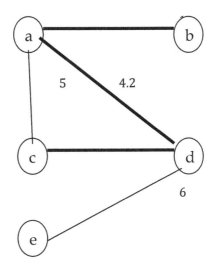

Forth iteration:

Next, the edges (a,c) is of weight 5, the minimum for the remaining edge. However, the edges (a,c) forms a cycle with two edges in E_g viz , (a,d) and (c,d). Hence (a,c) is not selected and hence not considered as a part of the to-be-found spanning tree.

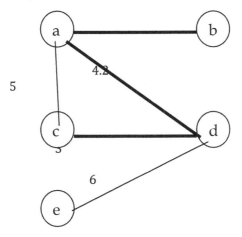

At the end of fourth iteration, the graph with selected edges in bold remains the same as at the end of the third iteration as shown below:

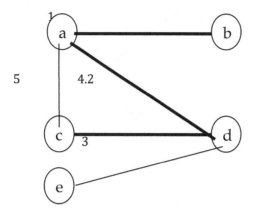

Fifth iteration-

Next, the edge (e, d), the only remaining edge that can be considered, is considered. As (e,d) does not form a cycle with any of the edges in E_g . Hence the edge (e,d) is put in Eg. The graph at this stage, with selected edge in bold is as follows:

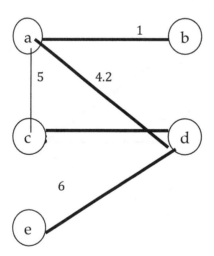

At this stage we find each of the vertices of the given is a vertex of some edges in Eg . further we observe that the edges in Eg, it is clear that the spanning tree is of minimum weight. Next we consider semi_formal definition of Krushal's algorithm.

ALGORITHM Spanning Krushal (G, E$_T$)

The algorithm constructs a minimum spanning tree by choosing successively edges of minimum weight out of the remaining edges.

The input to the algorithm is a connected graph G=(V, E) in which V is the set of vertices and E, the set of edges and weight of each edge is also given.
The output is the set of edges, denoted by E$_T$, which constitute a minimum spanning tree of G.

The variable edge counter is used to count the number of selected edges so far. Variable t is used to count the number of edges considered so far.

Arrange the edges in E in increasing order of the weight of edges. After the arrangement, the edges in order are labled as e1, e2, ...e$_{|E|}$

set ET:=⬚ ⬚ ⬚   ⬚ initialize the set of tree edges as empty.]
set EDGE_COUNTER :=0.   [initialize the counter to zero.]
set T:=0.   [initialize the number of processed edges as zero.]

[let N=number of edges in V]
Repeat steps while EDGE_COUNTER < N:

Set T:=T+1. [increment the counter for number of edges considered so far.]
       If the edges e$_t$ does not form a cycle with any subset of edges in E$_T$,
then:
              // if, e$_t$ alongwith edges earlier in E$_T$ do not form a cycle
              // then add e$_t$ to E$_T$ and increase edge counter
              E$_T$⬚ ⬚∪⬚ {e}.
              EDGE_COUNTER⬚ EDGE_COUNTER+1.
       [End of if structure.]
[End of loop.]
Return.

DIJKSTRA'S ALGORITHM (Shortest path algorithm):-

This is for finding the shortest path between two node in a weighted graph represented by a weight matrix.

That implementation was O(n^2), where n is the number of nodes in the graph.

```
For(all nodes i)
{
distance [i]=INFINITY;
perm[i]=NONMEMBER;
}
perm[s]=MEMBER;
distance[s]=0.
current=s;
while(current!=t)
{
dc=distance [current];
for(all nodes i that are successors of current)
{
newdist=dc+weight[current][i];
if (newdist<distance[i])
{
distance[i]=newdist; precede[i]=current;
}
}
k=the node k such that perm[k]==NONMEMBER and such that distance[k] is
smallest;
current=k;
perm[k]=MEMBER;
}
*p_d=distance[t];
```

At each stage dijkstra's algorithm selects a vertex v, which has the smallest d_v, among all the unknown vertices, and declares that the shortest path from s to v is known. The remainder of a stage consists of updating the value of d_w. $d_w = d_v + c_{v,w}$

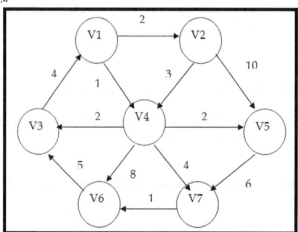

In the above graph G the third configuration, assuming that the start nods is v. The selected is v_1 with path length 0. This vertex is marked known. Now that v_1 is known, some entries need to be adjusted. The vertices adjacent to v_1 and v_4. Next v4 is selected and marked known. Vertices v6, v7 are adjacent and it turns out the all require adjusting.

v	Known	dv	Pv
v1	1	0	0
v2	0	2	v1
v3	0	∞	0
v4	0	1	v1
v5	0	∞	0
v6	0	∞	0
v7	0	∞	0

After v1 is declared knonwn

v	Known	dv	pv
v1	1	0	0
v2	0	2	v1
v3	0	3	v4
v4	1	1	v1
v5	0	3	v4
v6	0	9	v4
v7	0	5	v4

After v4 is declared knonwn

V	Known	dv	pv
v1	1	0	0
v2	1	2	V1
v3	0	3	V4
v4	1	1	V1
v5	0	3	V4
v6	0	9	V4
v7	0	5	V4

After v2 is declared knonwn

v	Known	dv	pv
v1	1	0	0
v2	1	2	V1
v3	1	3	V4
v4	1	1	V1
v5	1	3	V4
v6	0	8	V3
v7	0	5	v4

After v5 is declared known

v	Known	dv	pv
v1	1	0	0
v2	1	2	v1
v3	1	3	v4
v4	1	1	v1
v5	1	3	v4
v6	0	6	v7
v7	1	5	V4

After v7 is declared known

v	Known	dv	pv
v1	1	0	0
v2	1	2	V1
v3	1	3	V4
v4	1	1	V1
v5	1	3	V4
v6	1	6	V7
v7	1	5	V4

After v7 is declared known and algorithm terminates.

Tries:-

In trie each node in the tree can contain m pointers, corresponding to the m possible symbols in each position of the key. Thus, if the keys were numeric, there would be 10 pointers in a node if strictly alphabetic, there would be 26.(There might also be an extra pointer corresponding to eok.

Or a flag with each pointer indicating that it pointed to a record rather than to a tree node.) A pointer in node is associated with a particular symbol value based on its position in the node that is the first pointer corresponds to the lowest symbol value, the second pointer to the second lowest, and so forth.

It is therefore unnecessary to keep the symbol values themselves in the tree. The number of nodes that must be accessed to find a particular key is log mn. A digital search tree implemented in this way is called tries.

A tries is useful when the set of keys is dense. So that most of the pointers in each node are used. When the key set is sparse, a trie wastes a large amount of space with large nodes that are mostly empty.

If the set of keys in a trie is known in advance and does not change, there are a number of techniques for minimizing the space requirements. One technique is to establish a different order in which the symbols of a key are used for searching.(so that, for example the third symbol of the argument key might be used to access the appropriate pointer in the trie root, the first symbol in level 1 nodes, and so forth.)

Another technique is to allow tire nodes to overlap each other, so that occupied pointers of node overlaps empty pointers of another.

Dictionaries:-

A dictionaries is a collection of elements each elements has a field called key and no two elements have the same key value. The operations to be performed on a dictionary are

1-   Insert an element with a specified key value.
2-   Search the dictionary for an element with a specified key value.
3-   Delete an element with a specified key value.

Symbol Table:-

An important part of any compiler is the construction and maintenance of a dictionary containing names and their associated values. Such a dictionary is also called a symbol table. In a typical compiler there may be several symbol table corresponding to variable names, labels, literals etc.

The constraints which must be considered in the design of symbol table are processing time and memory space. Usually there exist some inverse relationship between the speed of symbol table algorithm and the memory space it requires.

There are a number of phases associated with the construction of symbol table. The principal phases that are buildings and referencing. The building phase involves the insertions of symbols and their associated values into a table, while referencing is the fetching technique or accessing of values from a table.

The most straightforward method of accessing a symbol table is by using the linear search technique. This method involves arranging the symbols sequentially in memory via a vector or by using a simple linear linked list. An insertion is easily handled by adding the new element to the end of the list.

When it is desired to search then it is also easily found. It will take on the average, N/2 comparison to find a particular symbol in a table containing N entries. Another relatively simple method of accessing a symbol table is the binary search method.

The entires in the table are stored in alphabetical or numerically increasing order. In this technique to find any element, first search middle and then compare it to the element then the required item found, if match occur and if match does not occur then repeated the procedure on the second half. An average of $\log_2$ N comparison is required to locate an entry.

A general algorithm for entering a name into a symbol table is as follows.

1. compute the hash number.
2. Allocate a new node and set it fields.
3. If the equivalence class is empty then add node to the equivalence class return.
4. Repeat step 5 while a duplicate name is not found and the end of the equivalence list is not reached.
5. Obtain the next name in the equivalence class.
6. If a duplicate name was not found then add the node to the equivalence class .
7. Return.

CHAPTER
∞ **12** ∞
(ALGORITHMS)

Introduction-

Algorithm No. 1: Sum of two numbers

1. Read A and B.
2. Set SUM:=A + B.
3. Write SUM.
4. Exit.

Algorithm No. 2: Maximum of two numbers

1. Read A and B.
2. If A > B, then:
        Set MAX:=A.
    Else:
        Set MAX:=B.
    [End of If structure]
3. Write MAX.
4. Exit

Algorithm No. 3: Maximum of three numbers.

1.   Read A , B,C.
2.   If A > B, then:
            If A > C, then:
                   Set MAX:=A.
            Else:
                   Set MAX:=C.
            [End of If structure]
        Else:
            If B > C, then:
                   Set MAX:=B.
            Else:
                   Set MAX:=C.
        [End of If Structure]
3.   Write MAX.
4.   Exit.

Algorithm No. 4:
To input percentage from user and print the grade.(Using Else if)

1.   Read P.
2.   If P>=90, then:
            Set GRADE:='A'.
        Else If P >= 70, then:
            Set GRADE := 'B'.
        Else if P>=50, then:
            Set GRADE:='C'.
        Else:
            Set GRADE:='F'.
        [End of If Else Structure].
3.   Write GRADE.
4.   Exit

Algorithm No. 5: To print the series 1 to N using *for loop*.

1.   Read N.
2.   Repeat Step 3 for I:=1 to N:
3.   Write I.
        [End of Step 2 loop]
4.   Exit.

Algorithm No. 6: To print the series 1 to N using while *loop*.

1.   Read N.
2.   Set I:= 1
3.   Repeat Step 4 and 5 While I<= N:
4.   Write I.
5.   Set I:=I+1.
        [End of Step 3 loop]
6.   Exit.

Algorithm No. 7: To print the series 1 to N using *do while loop*.

1.   Read N.
2.   Set I:=1.
3.   Write I.
4.   Set I:=I + 1.
5.   if I<=N, then: goto step3.
6.   Exit.

Algorithm No. 8: Convert decimal number to binary equivalent.

1.   Read N.
2.   Set B:=0.
3.   Set I:=0.
4.   Repeat step 6 to 9 While N>=0
5.   Set N:= N/2.
6.   Set B:= B + 10^i * Remainder   [this part will take care of reversing the accumulated remainders].
7.   Set I:=I+1.
8.   Write B.
9.   Exit

Algorithm No. 9:Reverse the digits of given n digit numbers.

1.   Read N.
    2. Set REV:=0.
    3. Repeat steps 5 and 6 While N>=0.
    4. Set N:=N/10.
    5. Set REV:= REV *10 + remainder.
    6. Print the value of REV.
    7. Exit.

Algorithm No. 10: To verify whether a given number is prime or not.

1. Read N.
2. Set I:=2 and PRIME =1.
3. Repeat Steps 4 while I<=N/2
4. If(N % I=0)
   >   Set PRIME:=0. and exit the loop structure.
   Else:
   >   Set I:= I+ 1.
   [End of If Structure.]
   [End of While loop]
5. If PRIME=1, then:
   >   Print the number is prime.
   Else
   >   Print the number is not prime.
6. Exit.

Algorithm No. 11: Linear search in an array.

Algorithm No. 12: Calculate factorial using function.

1. Read N.
2. ANS=FACT (N).
3. Write ANS.
4. Exit

[This procedure is used to calculate the factorial of N]

1. Set ANS:=1
2. Repeat step 3 for I:=N to 1
3. Set ANS:= ANS* I
4. [End of Step 3 loop]
5. Return ANS.
6. Exit.

CHAPTER
∞ 13 ∞
(UNSOLVED PRACTICAL PROBLEMS)

Introduction-

1.   A phone number such as (011)711 8802 can be thought of as having three parts: the area code(011), the exchange(711), and the number (8802).write a program that uses a structure to store these three parts of a phone number separately. Call the structure phone. Create an array to store 20 records of its member wherein each record stores the memberno, member name and phone number of phone type. Have the user input the information for all records and then display the entire information on the screen.

2.   Create a structure called volume that uses three variables (length, width, height) of type distance (feet and inches) to model the volume of a room. read the three dimensions of the room and calculate the volume it represents, and print out the result. The volume should be in (feet)^3 form i.e., you will have to convert each dimension in to feet and fractions of foot. For instance, the length 12 feet 6 inches will be 12.5 feet.

SERIOUS NOTE:
     In this book WAP means "Write a Program" Okay !!

3. Declare a structure to represent a complex number (a number having a real part and imaginary part).write a c program to add two complex numbers.

4. Declare a structure to represent a complex number (a number having a real part and imaginary part).write a c program to subtract two complex numbers.

5. Declare a structure to represent a complex number (a number having a real part and imaginary part).write a c program to multiply two complex numbers.

6. Declare a structure to represent a complex number (a number having a real part and imaginary part).write a c program to divide two complex numbers.

7. WAP to record score of a cricket match. one array stores information of batting team such as batsman's name, run scored, indication if out mode by which out along with total runs, overs played, total overs and extras. The other array stores information about bowling team such as bowler's name, overs bowled, maiden overs, runs given and wickets taken. The program reads in the above information and depending upon the user's choice, it displays either the batting team's information or the bowling team's information.

8. WAP to prepare the invoice from the following data: customer number, customer name and address, data of sale, description, quantity, unit price, discount percentage, sales tax percentage.

9. WAP to prepare and print payroll (payslip) of a group of employees for a particular month of the year. the employee information contains the following items: name and designation of employee, basic pay(bp),special pay(sp), contribution to general provident fund(pf),contribution to group scheme(gis),income tax deduction(it),city compensatory allowance(cca)= rs. 250,dearness allowance(da)=114% for basic pay < rs. 3500 85% for basic pay > 3500 and < 6000   74% for basic pay pay > 6000 house rent allowance(hra)=rs. 250.00 for basic pay < rs. 1500 rs. 450.00 for basic pay > 1499 and 2800 rs. 800.00 for basic pay > 2799 and < 3500   rs. 1000.00 for basic > 3499. The program computes the above quantities, gross pay, total deductions net pay and prints in a specified format. (hint: gross=bp+sp+hra+da+cca   net=gross-deductions(i.e.,pf+gis+it) make use of structures and arrays in the program.

10.   WAP to store 20 records containing country, capital and name of its president. the president name it is a record containing last name, first name, preface(mr, miss, mrs.).the program should display the entire record whenever the country name or capital is given.

11.   Suppose a store has a number of items in their inventory and that each item is supplied by almost two suppliers. WAP to store details of 20 items in an array and then print it.

12. An array stores details of 25 students (rollno, name, marks in three subjects).WAP to create such an array and print out a list of students who have failed in more than one subjects. assume 40% as pass marks.

13.   WAP to calculate income tax of a group of employee from the following data. Total income, life insurance premiums (lic),unit-linked insurance plan (ulip),provident fund(pf),post-office cumulative time deposit(ctd), national saving certificates(nsc) Assume the following norms for the calculation of income tax: a tax total income slab rates of income tax
upto 35000   nil
from 35001 to 60000   20%
from 60001 to 120000   30%
120000 and above   40%

   b exemptions contributions to lic, gpf, ppf, ulip, nsc, ctd etc, are exempt from paying income tax subject to a maximum of rs. 120000 is admissible.

14.   A linear array of size 50 stores following information's: name of the country, country's capital and per capita income of the country. write a complete program in c to do the following:

   a) to read a country's name and display capital and per-capita income.

   b) to read name of the capital city and displays country's name and displays country's name and per capital income. display an error message incase of an incorrect input.

15.   WAP using structure to store price list of 50 items and to print the largest price as well as the sum of all prices.

16.   WAP in c using structure to simulate result preparation system for 20 students. the data available for each student includes rollno, name and marks in 3 subjects.

The percentage marks and grade are to be calculated from the above information, the percentage marks are the average marks are the average marks and the grade is calculated as

follows:

% marks	grade
< 50	'f'
>=50 < 60	'd'
>=60 < 75	'c'
>=75 < 90	'b'
>=90 < 100	'a'.

17.   WAP a c program to simulate an arithmetic calculator for integers. the program should be able to produce the last result calculated and the number of arithmetic operations performed so far. any wrong operations is to be reported.

18.   WAP to make a structure named "student" having following as structure member:1) name 2) roll-no 3) marks of three subjects viz. English, hindi, maths. do the following operations using the structure:

a) accept name, roll no and marks in three subjects.
b) calculate total and percentage.
c) show the information on the screen in given below format XYZ school half yearly examination

Name: roll no:
Marks in Hindi:
Marks in English:
Marks in Maths:

Total marks: per:

19.   WAP to make a structure "contestant" for a beauty contest in which check the following condition & accept details for 5 contestants only if they satisfy following criteria:
a) if age is between 18 to 20
b) Weight is between 45 to 60
c) Qualification is graduate

Structure members are: 1) Name 2) Age 3) Weight 4) Qualifications-->
1. Below graduate 2. Graduate 3. Postgraduate. Now display the details of all 5 contestant in tabular manner.

20.   WAP to make structure "stock". Accept details of 10 stock items. The structure members are :1) item_name 2) item_code 3) rate 4) qty_in_ stock 5) amount. now ask of the user item code which he want to see, search it display it if it exit otherwise give appropriate message.

21.   WAP to create a structure to specify data on students given below: roll number, name, department, course, year of joining assume that there are not more than 450 students in the college. do the following operations using the structure:

a) print names of all students who joined in a particular year.
b) print the data on a student whose roll number is given.

21.   Create a structure to specify data of customers in a bank. the data to be stored is: account number, name ,balance in account. assume maximum of 200 customers in the bank. do the following operations using the structure:

a) to print the account number and name of each customer with balance RS. 100.if a customer requests for withdrawal or deposit, it is given in the form: acct. no, amount,(1 for deposit,0 for withdrawal)

b) to give a message, "the balance is insufficient for the specified withdrawal".

22.   An automobile company has serial numbers for engine parts starting from aa0 to ff9. The other characteristics of parts be specified in a structure are: year of manufacture, material and quantity manufactured. now, do the following:

a) specify a structure to store information corresponding to a part.

b) WAP to retrieve information on parts with serial numbers between bb1 and cc6.

23.   A record contains name of cricketer, his age, number of test matches that he has played and the average runs that he has scored in each test match. create an array of structures to hold records of 20 such cricketers and then write a program to read these records and arrange them in ascending order by average runs.

24.   Create a structure to represent a book in a library. It include the following members: book number, book name, author, publisher, price, no. of copies, no. Of copies issued. now do the following operations using the structure:

25.
        a) to assign initial values.
        b) to issue a book after checking for its availability.
        c) to return a book.
        d) to display book information.

26. Create a structure to represent bank account of 10 customers with the following data members: name of the depositor, account number, type of account (s for saving and c for current account),balance amount. now, do the following operations using the structure:

a) To initialize data members
b) To deposit money.
c) For withdrawal of money after checking the minimum balance(minimum balance is rs.1000).
d) To display the data members.

26. Create a structure to represent batsman in a cricket team. it include the following members: first name, last name, runs made, number of fours, number of sixes. now do the following operations using the structure:

a) to assign the initial values.
b) to update runs made(it should simultaneously update fours and sixes, if required).
c) to display the batsman's information.
make appropriate assumptions about access labels.

27. Create a structure to represent bowlers in a cricket team. include the following members: first name, last name, overs bowled, number of maiden overs, runs given, wickets taken. now do the following operations using the structure:

a) to assign the initial values
b) to update the information
c) to display the bowler's information.
make appropriate assumptions about access labels.

29. WAP to manage a room's statistics. the room structure includes the following members: length, width, height. now do the following operations using the structure:
a) to assign initial values.
b) to calculate area.
c) to display information (length, width, height & area).

30. Modify the above program so that length, width and height become the variable of structure distance that includes: meters, centimeters.

31. Let itemlist be a linear array of size n (where n is a user input) where each element of the array contains following fields: item, code, item price, quantity. declare a structure with itemlist as data member and perform the following operations:

a) appending an item to the list.
b) given the itemcode, delete an item from the list.
c) printing the total value of the stock.

32.   WAP to handle 10 account holders. the program should use the structure as defined in q.33.make necessary changes in the class definition - if required.

33.   Write a structure to represent a vector (1-d numeric array).now do the following operations using this structure:

a) for vector creation
b) for modification of a given element.
c) for displaying the largest value in the vector.
d) for displaying the entire vector.
e) for adding two vectors and displays the resultant vector.
WAP using this structure.

34.   Create two structures mc and fi which store the value of distances. mc stores distances in meters and centimeters whereas fi stores in feet and inches. WAP that reads value for variables of both the structures and can add one variable of mc with an variable of fi.

35.   Imagine a ticket selling both at a fair. people passing by are required to purchase a ticket. A ticket is priced as RS. 2.50/-. The booth keeps track of the number of people that have visited the booth, and of the total amount of money collected. Model this ticket selling booth with a structure called ticbooth including following members: number of people visited, total amount of money collected. Now do the following operations:

a) to assign initial values (assign 0 to both data members).
b) to increment only people total in case ticket is not sold out
c) to increment people total as well as amount total if a ticket is sold out.
d) to display the totals.
e) to display the number of tickets sold out(a tricky one).
WAP to include this structure.

36.   WAP to perform various operations on a string structure without using language supported built-in string functions. The operations on a structure are:
        a) Read a string.
        b) Display the string.
        c) Reverse the string.
        d) Copy the string into an empty string.
        e) Concatenate two strings.

37.   WAP to process the sales activity for 20 salesman. Each salesman deals in separate product and is assigned an annual target. At the end of the month, his monthly sale is added into the sales till date. At the end of the year, his commission is calculated as follows: if sales made is more than target then the commission is 25% of the extra sales made + 10% of the target if sales made is equal to the target then the commission is 10% of the target. Otherwise commission is zero.

38.   A bookshop maintains the inventory of books that are being sold at the shop. The list includes details such as author, title, price, publisher and stock position. Whenever a customer wants a book, the sales person inputs the title and author and the system searches the list and displays whether it is available or not.

       If it is not, an appropriate message is displayed. If it is, then the system displays the book details and requests for the number of copies required. If the requested copies are available, the total cost of the required copies is displayed, otherwise the message "sorry! These many copies are not in stock" is displayed. Design a system using a structure called stock. This program includes the following operations:

             a) The price gets updated as and when required.
             b) The stock value of each book should be automatically updated as soon as transaction is completed.
             c) The total number of books (titles) sold get displayed (along with total sales (in RS.) As and when required.

39.   WAP to print the score board of a cricket match in real time. The display should contain the batsman's name, runs scored, indication if out, mode by which out, bowler's score (overs played, maiden overs, runs given, wickets taken).as and when a ball is thrown, the score should be updated.(hint: use separate arrays to store batsman's and bowlers, information).

40.   WAP to prepare the invoice from the following data: customer name, customer name, customer address, date of sale, item no, item description, quantity sold, unit price of item, discount percentage and sales tax percentage.

       Note: identify different structures possible here.

41.   A college maintains a list of its students graduating every year. at the end of the year, the college produces a report that lists the following:

year:
number of working graduates   :
number of non-working graduates :
details of the top-most scorer
name   :
age   :
subject   :
average marks :
x% of the graduates this year are non-working and n % are first divisioners.

WAP for it that uses the following structure path:
person -----> student ------>   graduate student
(name, age)   (roll no, average marks)   (subject, employed)
the data members of these structures have seen shown in the parenthesis.

42.   WAP that reads several different names and rearranges the names
       into alphabetical order, and then writes out the alphabetized list.
       make use of structure variables within the program.

43.   Assume that a bank maintains two kinds of accounts for customers,
       one called as savings account and the other as current account. the
       savings account provides compound interest and withdrawal
       facilities but not cheque book facility.

       The current provides cheque book facility but no interest. Current
       account holders should also maintain a minimum balance and if the
       balance falls below this level, a service charge is imposed. create a
       structure account that stores customer name, account number and
       opening balance. from this derive the structures current and savings
       to make them more specific to their requirements. now do the
       following tasks:

       a) deposit an amount for a customer and update the balance.
       b) display the account details.
       c) compute and deposit interest.
       d) withdraw amount for a customer after checking the balance and
       update the balance.
       e) check for the minimum balance(for current account holders),
       impose penalty, if necessary, and update the balance.

44.   WAP defining an union which can hold an "integer" or "float" string.
       define a variable "union type" to keep track of the type of data stored
       in the union. write a function to print the value stored in the union.

45. WAP to define a union of type "ans" containing two members-an integer quantity and a floating quantity. Compute the average and standard deviation of the numbers and print them.

46. WAP for the following: track sales for a used-car business with 12 brands in stock, each with an integer code, and generate a daily report that indicates
   a) inventory by brand at day's start.
   b) total cars sold by brand at day's end.
   c) sales as a percentage of inventory, by brand.
   (assume all cars have the same price)
   sample input:

car brand no.	No. Of cars in stock	No. Of cars sold
1	10	0
2	12	0
3	13	6
---	---	---
12	30	0

   Sample output:
   Brand #: 1
   ----
   brand #: 3
   inventory at day's start: 23
   total sales: 6
   inventory at day's end: 17
   sales as percentage of inventory: 26.086957
   ----

47. WAP that can maintain the name, roll number and marks of a class of students. the size of the class is variable. include functions to compute the average marks of the class.

48. WAP to read in a string and output the frequency, of each character in that string.

49. WAP to read in a string and output the frequency of each word in that string.

50. A company pays normal wage for work during weeks days from monday to friday and 1.5 times wage for work on saturday and sunday. given data in the following form:
   employee number, wage/hour, hours worked on monday, hours on tuesday,.., hours on sunday.

   WAP to write out the employee number and weekly wages. use enumerated data type in your program.

51. Define a structure for a student having name, roll number and marks obtained in six subjects. assume that "all students" is an array of students. WAP to print the name and roll numbers of the students who have secured highest marks in each subject.

52. Define a structure "mca2_oops" which has the members: entry_no, marks, marks_minor, marks_ major, total. WAP for initialize the variables of objects, finding the total marks which is sum of marks_major and marks_minor. This program will handle 30 students and displaying their marks.

53. Create a structure of big cities bigcity of india,the data member of the structure are name of the city,std code(say for calcutta std code is 033) etc.WAP which interactively ask the name abd addresss,local phone number of residents and print in the following format:
1. Name:s.p.rama rao   2. Address:3/2 apc road
3. Pincode no.: 700052   4. Phone no: (033)-4347270

Advise - Other Best Selling Java Books (Paperback & Digital PDF)

Top 10 Java Books **for Students & Professionals-Search on Amazon.com or Google Play & Google Books. (Book Pages – 900, Total Chapters 30)**

1. Java Teach Yourself Core Java in 21 Days. 2014,
   ISBN- 978-1499643015.
2. Beginning Programming with Java.: Easy Version. 2014
   ISBN- 978-1499643039.
3. Core Java Professional : Learn Java Step By Step With Fun.
   ISBN - 978-1499651027.
4. Effective Core Java.: The Complete Core Reference.
   ISBN - 978-1499642582.
5. Java Brainstorming.: Special Beginners Edition 2014.
   ISBN - 978-1499651119.
6. Java Power To you.: Special Beginner's Edition 2014.
   ISBN - 978-1499651621.
7. Java, Brain-Washer.: Special Beginners Edition 2014.
   ISBN - 978-1499651324.
8. Thinking in Java.: Special Beginner's Edition 2014.
   ISBN - 978-1499651478.
9. Effective Core Java.: The Complete Core Reference.
   ISBN - 978-1499642582.
10. JAVA The HARDER BETTER FASTER STRONGER. 978-1499651614

Best Java Interview Books on Amazon.com or Google Books / play. Search with Book ISBN Or Author Name- Harry H Chaudhary.

1. Cracking The Java Coding Interview Hand Book 2014.
2. Java Interview Questions & Answers 2013-2014 Edition.
3. Java Interview Made Easy.
4. Technical Interview Made Easy.

Best Data Structure and Algorithms Books List Search on Amazon.com or Google Play & Google Books. Search with Book ISBN Or Author Name- Harry H Chaudhary.

1. Data Structures And Algorithms.: Made Easy.
   ISBN- 978-1495996016
2. Algorithms, Professional Edition.: Beginner's Guide.
   ISBN- 978-1500137274
3. Thinking In Data Structures and Algorithms.:
   ISBN-978-1500137281

Best C & C++ Books Search on Amazon.com or Google Play & Google Books. Search with Book ISBN Or Author Name- Harry H Chaudhary.

1. C Programming Professional.: Sixth Edition 2014 For Beginner's.
   ISBN-: 978-1495995767

2. C++ Programming Professional. ISBN- 978-1495995552

Best C# Programming Books on Amazon.com or Google Books / play. Search with Book ISBN Or Author Name- Harry H Chaudhary.

1. How to Become a C# Programmer. ISBN: 978-1500193683.

2. Head First C# . ISBN: 978-1500193690.

3. Effective C# : ISBN: 978-1500193614.

4. C# Professional : ISBN: 978-1500193874.

We Want to Hear from You!

Search on Google Books or Google play- search this book- *Cracking the Java Coding Interview By Harry H. Chaudhary, This book cointains 1000+ Java Interview Questions & Answers and explains each step of Technical Interview.* Another **Best Selling Java Book "Core Java Professional" Cointains 900 pages with 30 Chapters with live software Project covers all Basic to Advance Java Topics.** Download Digital Edition of this book with 5.99 USD Only Limited time offer for serious Readers. First Download Free Demo then Purchase with $5.99

As the reader of this book, you are our most important critic and commentator. We value your opinion and want to know what we're doing right, what we could do better, what areas you'd like to see us in correction or publish in, and any other words of wisdom you're willing to pass our way.

You can email or write me directly to let me know what you did or didn't like about this book—as well as what we can do to make our books stronger.

Please note that I cannot help you with technical problems related to the topic of this book, and that due to the high volume of mail I receive, I might not be able to reply to every message. When you write, please be sure to include this book's title and author as well as your name and phone or email address. I will carefully review your comments and share them with the author (Myself) and editors who worked on this book.

One more thing don't forget to give us star Reviews rate comments on Amazon.com **Please** Visit on Amazon.com or other website from where you purchased this book. and Write your own customer Review Rate (Stars) from your heart to our Book and Comments that will help us to improve this book data to make better and better for future

I did hardwork and I Spent several hours to make this book, atleast I can expect one customer review from you, I hope this book helped you a lot , please share this book with other students and tell your college friends about this book **but please suggest to consider buying your own copy from pothi.com (pdf) or createspace.com store (paperback), lulu.com, smashwords.com, amazon.com (kindle & paperback) or google books (digital) , google Play Store (digital)**

Both Physical Paperback and Digital Editions Are also Available on Amazon.com And Createspace Book Store , but on **google books (digital) , google Play Store (digital)** & pothi.com just Order today **and Get a Discounted digital Copy** with very low price. I would like to suggest you, buy paperback edition for better understanding, search this book's paperback edition on amazon.com with following ISBN Numbers-**ISBN10: 1500137138.** *ISBN-13:* **978-1500137137.**

CPSIA information can be obtained at www.ICGtesting.com
Printed in the USA
LVOW04s2125091014

408072LV00033B/872/P

9 781500 137137